Oklahoma Hiking Trails

Oklahoma Hiking Trails

Kent F. Frates and Larry Floyd

Maps and Photographs by Larry Floyd

University of Oklahoma Press : Norman

This book is published with the generous assistance of the Wallace C. Thompson Endowment Fund, University of Oklahoma Foundation.

Design: Eric H. Anderson

Frontispiece: View from the Skyline Trail in Beavers Bend State Park, near Broken Bow.

Library of Congress Cataloging-in-Publication Data

Frates, Kent F.

Oklahoma hiking trails / Kent F. Frates and Larry Floyd; maps and photographs by Larry Floyd.

p. cm.

ISBN 978-0-8061-4141-1 (pbk. : alk. paper)

1. Hiking—Oklahoma—guidebooks. 2. Trails —Oklahoma— Guidebooks. 3. Oklahoma—Guidebooks. I. Floyd, Larry (Larry C.), 1952–. II. Title.

GV199.42.O5F73 2010

917.66—dc22

2010002149

The paper in this book meets the guidelines for permanence and durability of the Committee on Production Guidelines for Book Longevity of the Council on Library Resources, Inc. ∞

1 2 3 4 5 6 7 8 9 1

Contents

Acknowledgments

We would like to acknowledge our friends who accompanied us on many of our hikes: Howard Lucero, Tracy Habluetzel, Bill Weeks, Sharon Brywczynski, Johnny Puckett, and Rita Hejny.

We would also especially like to acknowledge Kirk Bjornsgaard, our original editor at the University of Oklahoma Press, who appreciated the merit of this book and helped to ensure its publication. Unfortunately, Kirk passed away before the book was finished.

Getting Started

What is it that makes hiking such a pleasurable outdoor activity? First of all, a hike can be many things—from a pleasant stroll through the countryside to a rugged outdoor trek. This diversity makes it appealing to a wide range of people. Some want a healthy activity for fitness, while others seek adventure. All can find satisfaction in the right hike. Even an experienced hiker usually feels at least a little sense of adventure when setting out.

In our increasingly urban society, hiking also provides an escape from the noise, pace, and clutter of civilization. The quiet solitude of the woods offers relief from the pressures of a job and daily life in the city. Hiking Oklahoma's trails can also be a great way to see the state. From the high plains of Black Mesa to the pine forests of Beavers Bend State Park, the Sooner State stretches across miles of diverse territory that can best be appreciated on foot. The prospect of seeing interesting birds and animals—including the possibility of a bear or a mountain lion—adds another incentive to hit the trail.

The temperate climate in Oklahoma allows hiking year-round. We hope this book takes you down pathways you have never traveled. Before starting, however, you should have the right equipment and make the proper preparations. Although hiking is not inherently dangerous, you soon acquire a healthy respect for Mother Nature and learn to be prepared for varied conditions, including Oklahoma's unpredictable weather. The following pages offer tips on getting started in what can be a lifelong activity.

Equipment and Other Useful Items

Boots. If you're thinking about going hiking, the first and most important item you need is a sturdy and comfortable pair of boots—not running shoes. Running shoes are for running; boots are for hiking. You need the support and the hard soles of boots to withstand the ups and downs, rocks, roots, and irregular surfaces encountered on a hike. Some experienced hikers prefer trail running shoes, but these do not provide the support or protection afforded by boots.

In today's market you have a wide selection of boots, from high-tops to three-quarters to low-tops, in a variety of weights, styles, and compositions. If you're going to be day hiking and not backpacking, you won't need a really heavy boot. A sturdy, lightweight boot is just fine. Many good ones are available, including those made by Montrail, Nike, Vasque, and Salomon. Buying a well-made pair of boots is not the time to save money. Your feet will thank you for purchasing quality footwear. Cheap boots are a false economy: good boots last a lot longer than cheaper ones.

Buying your boots, however, is just a start. You need to break them in before you hit the trail. Walk in your neighborhood or in the park, but be sure to wear them until they become comfortable. It's not just your boots that need breaking in but your feet as well. To avoid blisters, your feet should be toughened up before you take a hike. Although this requires a fair amount of walking in your boots, it is well worth your time.

Socks. Socks deserve special attention as well. Forget about cotton socks: cotton is not your friend. It can become wet and stay wet for a long time. Wool and synthetic fibers dry quickly and make much better hiking socks. You may also want to experiment with wearing a sock liner, especially if you are prone to blisters.

Rain gear. Next on your shopping list should be rain gear. A full waterproof rain suit, including jacket and pants, is important. Be sure that what you buy is waterproof, not water resistant. Don't learn the difference the hard way—when you're five miles from the trailhead in the middle of a cold, driving rainstorm. Quality lightweight rain gear is available from Marmot, Patagonia, Royal Robbins, and North Face, to name a few.

Pack. You also need a pack. If you are just day hiking, don't take a heavy backpack. Stay light as the day grows long, you don't want to carry extra weight. Packs with built-in water bladders or with water-bottle holders can provide a quick drink without having to stop and take off your pack.

Clothing. Just about any clothing that fits and is comfortable works, although once again cotton's water-absorbing quality makes it least preferable. The bears won't be impressed with your brand-new outfit anyway. Since hiking year-round is possible in Oklahoma, you need to adapt to the weather. In colder weather a number of light layers are preferable to a heavy coat. This allows easier adjustment to weather changes and heat gain from exercise.

Hydration. Water becomes vital on a vigorous day hike—and more than you think you need. Sports drinks are also good, particularly on hot days. Insulated water bottles can be used in summer to keep your water cool, and hard-plastic bottles can protect against freezing during winter hikes. Various purification systems are available to filter water from streams or lakes, but you can usually carry enough water to avoid needing to purify water. In any event, be sure to keep yourself well hydrated during your hike by drinking periodically.

Sunscreen. The Oklahoma sun can be brutal in summer, so sunscreen should always be applied before a hike and sometimes during it. Try to find sports sunscreen that does not wash off with your sweat and irritate your eyes.

Hiking poles. You should consider hiking (or trekking) poles. These poles, which resemble ski poles, are especially useful on steep ascents and descents. They are designed to telescope from short to long and can be secured to your backpack when not in use. Increasingly popular, particularly on long, steep hikes, they distribute your weight, allowing you to use your arms for strength and balance, and can be used for support when resting.

Other items. Some other items should be included, depending on the length and type of hike. Keep food light. Energy bars and gels are a good source and don't weigh much or take up much room in your pack. Salty snacks like pretzels, peanuts, or chips are good on hot days. Other items to carry are a pocketknife, first-aid kit, compass, and global positioning system (GPS)—and toilet paper. For safety purposes, a cell phone is a good idea. Be sure it's fully charged.

Trail Tips

Finding the trailhead. This may sound odd to those of you who haven't done much hiking, but it needs to be said: the most difficult part of the hike is often just finding the trailhead. Any experienced hiker can tell horror stories of trips up and down back roads searching for a trailhead and false starts on what turned out to be no trail at all. In this book we have tried to give a precise description of the way to the trailhead (TH) along with a GPS reading of its location. Still, if you are going on one of the true wilderness hikes in this book—especially in southeastern Oklahoma—it's a good idea to scout out the trailhead in advance or go with someone who has previously been on that trail.

Hiking alone. Many hiking guides recommend against solo hiking. This is the safest route to take, of course, and is recommended. On the other hand, most of the trails in Oklahoma are not at all dangerous. It would be a shame to deprive yourself of a good hike just because no one is available to accompany you. If you hike by yourself, let someone know where you are going, sign the register (if one exists) at the trailhead, and take your cell phone.

Stream crossing. Most experienced hikers simply wade on through and let their boots dry as they walk. Waterproofing can be applied to keep most of the moisture from penetrating the boot leather. Some like to take off their boots and socks and wade across in rubber sandals. This can become a nuisance for repeated crossings. Most of the trails in Oklahoma require very few stream crossings, so this is probably not an issue unless a great deal of rain has fallen.

Maps and directions. Before you take off, it is a good idea to know where you are going and how to get back. Try to begin hiking on well-marked trails. It's also helpful to go with an experienced hiker. As you get more involved in hiking, you can learn to use topographic maps, a compass, and a GPS, but initially these aids should not be necessary.

Insects. Mosquitoes, flies, ticks, and other insects can be repelled by bug spray, at least to some extent. Almost no defense exists against the tenacious Oklahoma chigger, although the best protection against chiggers and ticks may be powdered sulfur spread liberally around your boot tops, ankles, and waistband. It is best to wear long pants even in the summer. Particularly in the summer, you should shed your clothes and shower vigorously as soon as possible after completing the hike. If you know you have been exposed to chiggers, bath water mixed with a cup or more of bleach should help. Also examine yourself thoroughly for ticks. If you find any, remove them immediately.

Poisonous snakes. Oklahoma does have its share of nasty snakes, including rattlesnakes, copperheads, and water moccasins. So hikers should be especially cautious in certain areas during the warm-weather months. If you are bitten and can receive medical attention quickly, most authorities agree that your best bet is to leave the bite untreated and let the health specialists take care of it. If out in the wilds and miles from the trailhead, you should consider use of a negative-pressure suction device, available for purchase at outfitters or on the Internet. Then get medical attention as quickly as possible.

Variable weather. Oklahoma is well known for its unpredictable weather. Like the Boy Scouts, you should be prepared when you go hiking. Take your rain gear even on a nice day. Every season has its challenges, so plan for them. In the hot summer months try to time your hike for the early morning or evening. Fall is one of the best times to hike. The weather is cooler and more consistent, with fewer storms. But you still should be prepared for a sudden storm or an extreme drop in temperature. Winter hiking has some significant advantages: virtually no bugs or snakes. But even in cold weather you lose fluids that need to be replaced. Spring brings lots of violent storms and quick weather changes. If lightning occurs, get rid of any metal objects such as hiking poles. When the storm is really bad, it is best to crouch down, away from trees.

These are some of the more salient considerations for hiking in Oklahoma. As you gain experience, you can customize your gear and adapt your habits to the kinds of hikes and areas that you prefer. With a minimum of expense, hiking can be a great way to enjoy the outdoors and maintain your health. We hope that this book will enhance your outdoor adventures on the trails of Oklahoma.

Criteria for the Selection of Trails

When we began work on this book, we established criteria for selecting trails to be included. Never intending to include every trail in the state that could be hiked, we wanted a variety of enjoyable and accessible trails spread across the state. Every trail (1) had to be open to the public; (2) had to be a defined trail with an identifiable beginning and end that can be followed without getting lost; and (3) had to offer a worthwhile hiking experience.

We made every effort to identify as many trails as possible. Although we may have missed a few, we believe that we located and hiked most of the worthwhile trails in the state. If you know of a trail that was not included, we probably hiked it and decided against it.

For the most part, trails primarily designed for equestrian use are not included. These trails generally provide poor hiking because the horse traffic keeps the trail torn up. The horse droppings also attract flies, mosquitoes, and other insects. These trails frequently traverse open fields and plains, which offer less interesting hiking. We also intentionally omitted all-terrain vehicle (ATV) trails: ATV trails are for ATVs, not hikers, and vice versa.

For each of these trails, we have listed the distance and identified whether it's an out-and-back, loop, or point-to-point configuration. We have also rated the difficulty of the trail as "easy," "moderate," or "strenuous." These ratings are subjective, and hikers may have varying opinions based on their level of fitness and experience. For most hikers, our "strenuous" hikes are exactly that. The difficult trails are only enjoyable if you are in good condition and well prepared. If you are in doubt about your hiking ability, we suggest that you try a "moderate" hike before attempting one that is rated "strenuous."

We tried to include trails all across the state, even though the greatest concentration of trails lies in the southeast. Additionally, we included urban trails as an aid to both local residents and out-of-state visitors. We also attempted to provide a guide to a wide variety of trails suitable for all levels of hikers, from novice to experienced. All of the hikes are day hikes, although many are suitable for backpacking and camping trips.

We would be remiss not to express a special word of thanks to the Oklahoma Earthbike Fellowship and the local bicycle clubs around the state. These off-road bike organizations are responsible for establishing and maintaining (through strictly voluntary efforts) a large number of trails that would not exist without their help. Although designed for off-road biking, trails such as Lake Arcadia, Bluff Creek, Clear Bay, Keystone, NuDraper, Lake McMurtry, Turkey Mountain, Roman Nose, and others are available for the enjoyment of hikers. The members of these biking organizations give many hours of their time to make these trails available to all of us.

A number of potentially good trails in the state have unfortunately fallen into disrepair, however, due to lack of funds and neglect. Wilderness trails do not take much maintenance, but they cannot be completely ignored. Storms, wind, fire, and deterioration from natural elements cause a variety of problems. Trees fall across the trail, sections of the trail wash away, signage can be destroyed, and a trail can simply be overgrown by weeds and grass.

All of us should encourage our local, state, and federal governments to allocate at least some funds to maintain our trails. It is truly sad to see a trail system fall into such disrepair that it becomes unusable for most hikers. The loss of a precious resource can be avoided by a minimal investment in time and money.

We hope that this book will be a useful resource for anyone interested in hiking in Oklahoma. It can certainly be updated and improved in the future. So if you have any corrections or suggestions, we welcome your comments. In the meantime, good hiking!

Best Trails

While hiking the trails described in this book, we were frequently asked which were Oklahoma's best trails. In answer to this question, we have selected six of our favorite trails. Although the majority are in the southeastern part of the state, excellent trails are scattered across Oklahoma, and we have chosen trails in several areas.

In choosing these trails we used a simple criterion: were the hikes truly enjoyable? In all cases, the trails selected were scenic, in reasonable condition, and of sufficient length for a good outing.

You may find other trails that you like better, but these are our picks.

Black Mesa Summit, 8.4 miles (out and back): This is a unique hike to Oklahoma's highest point through high desert terrain different from any other area of the state.

Charons Garden, 5 miles (out and back): The Charons Garden hike includes a boulder field and great views of the Wichita Mountains.

Old Military Road, 6.5 to 8 miles (one way): This trail up the side of Winding Stair Mountain offers great views along this historic route.

Winding Stair Campground to U.S. Hwy 259 (Ouachita Trail), 6.8 miles (one way): This is one of the prettiest hikes in the state, through a pine forest past the highest point on the Ouachita Trail. It is the best section of the trail in Oklahoma.

Greenleaf State Park, 10 miles (loop): This scenic up-and-down trail through dense woods along the shore of Greenleaf Lake offers a challenging hike in northeastern Oklahoma.

David Boren Hiking Trail, 12.5 miles of trails: This well-maintained trail system winds through the pine forest of southeastern Oklahoma, with great views of the Mountain Fork River. The trails are designed so that you can select a distance for your hike.

We hope you will have the chance to enjoy all of these trails. Every one offers a memorable outdoor experience.

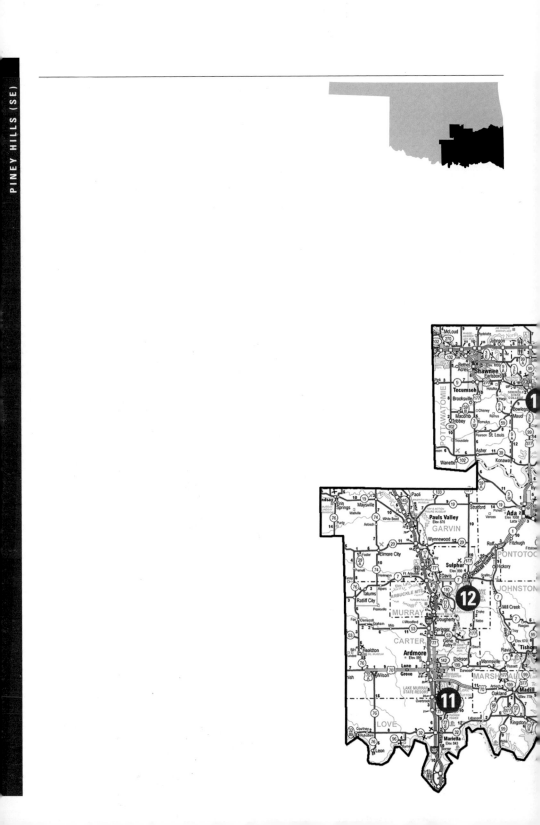

Piney Hills

Southeastern Oklahoma

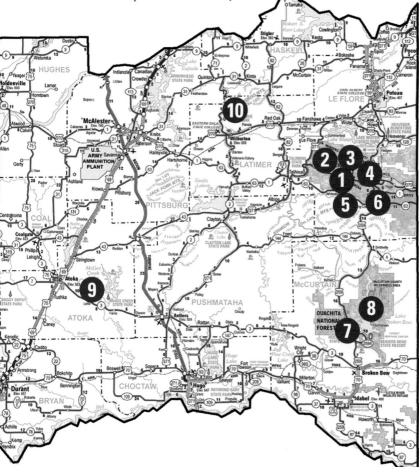

Piney Hills
Southeastern Oklahoma

The Indians were here first, hunting these forests where game was plentiful. Then came the French trappers, who left their mark with names like "Poteau" for a town and "Sans Bois" for a mountain range. Later, outlaws hid out in this lawless wilderness when it was part of Indian Territory. Now we are blessed with state parks and national forests that make a splendid setting for hiking.

Southeastern Oklahoma is a great place for camping, biking, horseback riding, canoeing, fishing, hunting, and kayaking as well as hiking. This part of the state has real mountains, dense pine forests, rivers, and creeks. The foliage is beautiful in the fall, and birds and wild animals abound year-round: deer, wild turkey, possums, raccoons, squirrels, and even some bears.

Make no mistake: this is still wilderness. Hiking in this area leads you through rocky, rugged country. To enjoy the trails in southeastern Oklahoma, you should be physically fit and prepared to deal with the terrain and the elements. If properly prepared, you are in for a treat. This is the best hiking area of the state, with varied terrain, beautiful scenery, and challenging routes.

❶ Ouachita National Recreation Trail

Among the many diverse hikes in southeastern Oklahoma, the premier venue is the Ouachita (pronounced Wash-i-taw) National Recreation Trail. The entire trail stretches 222 miles from Talimena State Park near Talihina, Oklahoma, to Pinnacle Mountain State Park just outside Little Rock, Arkansas. The part of the Ouachita Trail from the westernmost trailhead in Talimena State Park to the Arkansas line is 46.3 miles of excellent hiking, up and down mountains, across rivers, and through pine and oak forests. Since this book is a guide to Oklahoma trails, we have covered only this part. Several excellent guides treat the entire Ouachita Trail in great detail.

The entire section of the trail described here is in the Ouachita National Forest. It runs up and down the slopes and along the crest of the Ouachita Mountains, some of the highest peaks in the United States between the Rocky Mountains and the Appalachians. The Ouachitas are one of the few major U.S. mountain ranges that run east to west rather than north to south. The trail is open for hiking year-round but is probably best hiked in the late fall, when the temperature is generally moderate, although you should be careful during deer hunting season. In the summer the weather is sometimes brutally hot, and the ticks, chiggers, and mosquitoes can be obnoxious.

The Oklahoma section of the Ouachita Trail (which for much of its path parallels the Talimena Drive) has a number of access points. Thus the trail can be done as a through-hike for backpacking or broken down into day hikes of varying lengths. The sections from trailhead to trailhead can be hiked as out-and-back hikes or by use of a car drop. No matter how you undertake your hike, be sure to follow the simple safety rules of hiking, such as wearing proper clothing, taking plenty of water, and if possible hiking with a companion.

The trail sometimes grows faint or nonexistent but is marked by blue blazes. A number of area trails intersect the Ouachita Trail, and they are typically marked by white blazes. You must always look carefully for the blue blazes, no matter how confident of your direction. If you don't see any for a few minutes, you should backtrack until you pick up the trail again. In some places the trail is not well maintained and the blazes are faint or scattered, thus requiring constant attention to avoid losing the trail. Little danger exists on this trail. While sometimes rigorous, it provides a great outdoor experience.

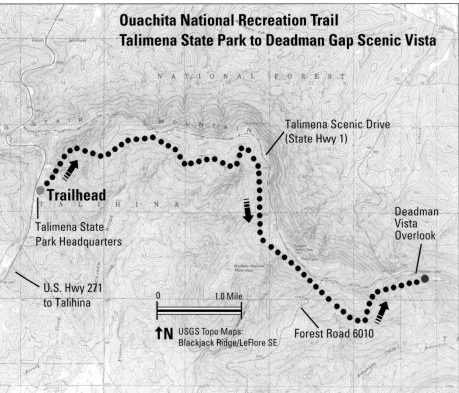

Ouachita National Recreation Trail
Talimena State Park to Deadman Gap Scenic Vista

Talimena Scenic Drive
(State Hwy 1)

Trailhead

Talimena State
Park Headquarters

Deadman
Vista
Overlook

U.S. Hwy 271
to Talihina

0   1.0 Mile

↑N USGS Topo Maps:
Blackjack Ridge/LeFlore SE

Forest Road 6010

❶ Talimena State Park to Deadman Gap

LENGTH: 8 miles one way

DIFFICULTY: Moderate/strenuous

USAGE: Hiking and mountain biking

TH GPS READING: N 34°47.007′ W 94°57.062′

Take U.S. Hwy 271 to the Talimena State Park west entrance, about one mile south of Talimena Drive (State Hwy 1). The trailhead begins at the edge of the woods near a camping/picnic area. The small park office as you enter has information and brochures.

Hikers follow the blue blazes through the heavy forest of pine and oak trees. The trail along this eight-mile stretch is occasionally rocky but easily navigable.

After less than a mile the trail crosses a small, usually dry creek before coming to a sign denoting the crossing of the Old Military Trail, which is marked by white blazes. Continuing along the Ouachita Trail, you can hear the sounds of motorcycles on the Talimena Drive (State Hwy 1) during fair weather. You can get occasional glimpses of forest vistas beyond the dense woods surrounding the trail. The mostly pine and oak trees display brilliant colors in the fall.

This leg of the Ouachita Trail can be used by hikers and mountain-bike enthusiasts, but its rocky surface discourages most riders. For the first few miles the trail mostly ascends but then levels off for a good distance. About three miles from the trailhead a beautiful vista opens. After about five miles you can make a short detour north onto the Talimena Drive to Panorama Vista.

The signs along the trail are in various states of disrepair. The blue blazes are rarely out of view, but vigilance is recommended to avoid wasteful detours.

At around six miles the trail crosses Forest Road 6010, and you can see the Talimena Drive to the left in the north. Signs are on both sides of this dirt road, but the one to note is to Deadman Gap, 2.3 miles ahead. Watch closely for the blue blazes as you cross this road, taking care not to follow a broad trail that proceeds straight ahead.

You're soon back into heavy pine and oak woods along this stretch of the trail. This is an especially scenic part of the woods, as you mostly descend along the trail. At just beyond seven miles you cross a rocky descending trail for off-road vehicles as you proceed north and east toward Deadman Gap. The last mile of this lovely forest brings you to a short ascent up to the Talimena Drive.

You're at the end of the first leg of the Ouachita Trail. The second leg begins across the highway and back into the woods.

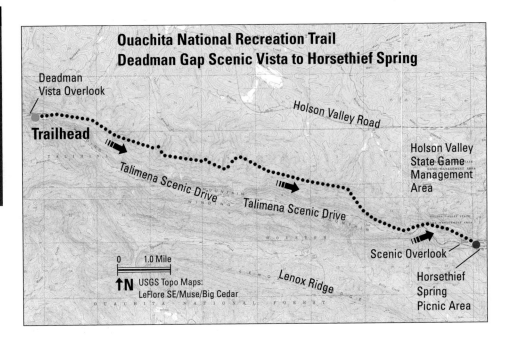

Ouachita National Recreation Trail
Deadman Gap Scenic Vista to Horsethief Spring

Deadman
Vista Overlook

Trailhead

Holson Valley Road

Talimena Scenic Drive

Talimena Scenic Drive

Holson Valley
State Game
Management
Area

Scenic Overlook

Horsethief
Spring
Picnic Area

Lenox Ridge

0   1.0 Mile

↑N USGS Topo Maps:
LeFlore SE/Muse/Big Cedar

❶ Deadman Gap to Horsethief Spring

LENGTH: 12 miles one way

DIFFICULTY: Strenuous

USAGE: Hiking

TH GPS READING: N 34°46.332' W 94°52.308'

The trailhead is located about a quarter-mile east of Deadman Gap Scenic Vista on the Talimena Drive (State Hwy 1), approximately seven miles east of the Information Center at the intersection of Hwy 1 and U.S. Hwy 271. It is on the north side of the road, marked by a hiker sign and blue blazes.

This section of the trail should only be attempted if you are doing a through-hike of the entire Ouachita Trail or are looking for an all-day adventure. It is definitely not for novices. Hiking this section means slow going over rough and rocky country, up and down the side of Winding Stair Mountain. At some points it is little more than directional bushwhacking: the trail itself is often faint or nonexistent, crossing boulder-strewn fields and rocky gulches and streambeds, and would only appeal to the most adventurous and experienced wilderness hikers. If you go, be sure to take plenty of water and watch for blue blazes on the trees, because it is easy to lose the trail.

The first quarter-mile of the trail is a steep descent down a rock-strewn hillside. At 0.7 mile the Boardstand Trail cuts off to the left down the mountain to an intersection with the Old Military Road Trail. Continue on the Ouachita Trail, which for the next two miles is rugged and ill-defined: most of the hiking is over rocks. At about 2.5 miles an even rockier patch extends for at least a quarter-mile. Be careful: watch closely for the blue blazes on the trees, because little or no evidence of the trail exists on the ground. If you are lost, backtrack to the last blue blaze. Use a compass or GPS and keep in mind the location of the Talimena Drive to help keep you oriented.

The trail continues from here with steep climbs and switchbacks up and down the side of Winding Stair Mountain. At 7.5 miles you cross a rockslide, which provides the opportunity for a great view looking north. Be sure to stop walking before taking in the scenery. You need to pay attention to your footing as you cross the rockslide.

In spite of the difficult nature of this hike, the scenery is beautiful, with oaks, pines, huckleberry bushes, and creeping vines. If you are patient and keep moving, you should have no trouble. By taking your time you can have an enjoyable outing, but don't expect to make good time: it is definitely slow going.

At about nine miles a sign indicates a trail (0.1 mile) to the Talimena Drive. This is a possible place to end your hike. The trail is marked a few yards from the Talimena Drive by two rock cairns that are difficult to see from the road but can be located with reference to the Cedar Lake Overview, which is 2.3 miles to the east.

After a little less than two miles a major trail intersection, the Horsethief Spring Trail, leads five miles to the north to Cedar Lake. Continue straight ahead on the Ouachita Trail. After another mile of hiking you come to an intersection with a spur trail up the hillside to your right to Horsethief Spring. The trail leads to a picnic area at the spring and marks the end of a long day of rigorous hiking.

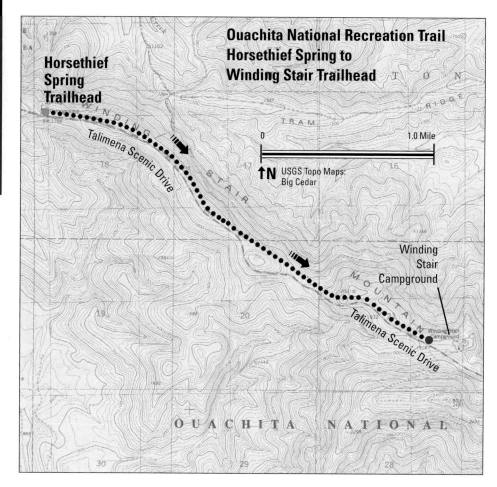

Ouachita National Recreation Trail
Horsethief Spring to
Winding Stair Trailhead

Horsethief Spring Trailhead

Talimena Scenic Drive

0   1.0 Mile

↑N USGS Topo Maps: Big Cedar

Winding Stair Campground

Talimena Scenic Drive

Winding Stair Campground

OUACHITA   NATIONAL

❶ Horsethief Spring to Winding Stair Trailhead

LENGTH: 4 miles one way

DIFFICULTY: Easy/moderate

USAGE: Hiking

TH GPS READING: N 34°44.270′ W 94°43.582′

The trailhead is at the Horsethief Spring picnic area, about 20 miles east of the intersection of State Hwy 1 and U.S. Hwy 271 and just off the Talimena Drive to the north. It is located at the north end of the paved parking lot and is well marked. The trailhead can be accessed from the Talimena Drive.

This section of the Ouachita Trail is a good day hike. It can be done as an out-and-back hike of eight miles or as a four-mile hike by dropping a car at the Winding Stair Trailhead, which is also accessed from the Talimena Drive. At Horsethief Spring outlaws like Belle Starr could find water for their horses even in dry periods. They also had a good view down the side of Winding Star Mountain and could see anyone who tried to approach their camp. This made an ideal hideout for horse thieves and gave the spring its name.

The trail begins with a short descent to the Ouachita Trail, which is marked with blue blazes as always. Turn right (east) and follow the trail as it parallels the Talimena Drive all the way to Winding Stair Campground. Unlike the hike from Deadman Gap to Horsethief Spring, this trail is fairly easy to walk and not difficult to follow. Several other trails and roads cross the Ouachita Trail, but in all cases you proceed straight ahead, following the blue blazes.

At 0.2 mile a trail intersects from the left, going downhill; this trail continues six miles to Cedar Lake as part of the Horsethief Spring trail loop. Continue straight ahead. At about two miles the trail crosses Forest Road 6014. The continuation of the trail on the other side of the road is well marked and easy to pick up. The trail leads down across a pretty little stream and then into pine forest. After another 0.5 mile the Billy Creek Trail intersects. It heads down the south side of the mountain to the Billy Creek Campground. As always on this section, keep going straight.

At 3.2 miles, just 0.8 mile from the Winding Stair Campground, the Mountain Top Trail crosses and proceeds to the right. Continue straight ahead and in a short time you reach the Winding Stair Trailhead. This location provides a good campsite, a parking area, and easy access to the Talimena Drive.

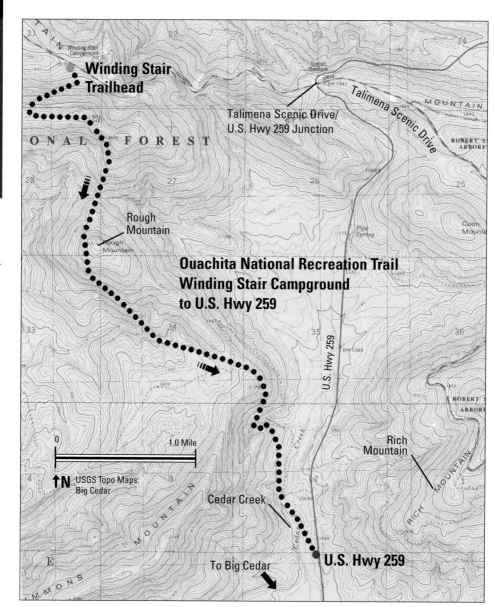

Winding Stair Campground

Winding Stair
Trailhead

Talimena Scenic Drive/
U.S. Hwy 259 Junction

Talimena Scenic Drive

MOUNTAIN

ONAL FOREST

ROBERT S
ARBORE

Rough
Mountain

Rough
Mountain

Coon
Mountain

Pipe
Spring

Ouachita National Recreation Trail
Winding Stair Campground
to U.S. Hwy 259

U.S. Hwy 259

ROBERT
ARBORE

Rich
Mountain

0   1.0 Mile

N USGS Topo Maps:
   Big Cedar

Cedar Creek

To Big Cedar

U.S. Hwy 259

❶ Winding Stair Campground to U.S. Hwy 259

LENGTH: 6.8 miles one way

DIFFICULTY: Moderate/strenuous

USAGE: Hiking and mountain biking

TH GPS READING: N 34°42.867′ W 94°40.786′

The trailhead begins across State Hwy 1 just south of Winding Stair Campground's Backpacker Camp.

Follow the blue blazes to the right of a metal roadblock, with two sets of signs at the trailhead. The trail begins a steady ascent into the woods as it winds south and west. After climbing steadily for nearly a mile, it levels off and turns back to the east for a short way.

Pine trees wall both sides of the trail here, and you can see a large rock cairn as the trail bends a little to the south. This marks the site of the remains of the old Winding Stair Fire Tower and the highest point on the Ouachita Trail: 2,451 feet above sea level.

The trail descends sharply from here for about a mile on a series of short switchbacks. A scenic but primitive campsite is located in a saddle at the bottom of the descent. This is one of the most secluded and tranquil points on the Ouachita Trail. In the fall the foliage is brilliant orange and yellow, and the scenery could match just about any setting along the storied Appalachian Trail.

The trail begins to ascend again, skirting the side of Rough Mountain. From about mile 3 to mile 4 the trail follows a wide ridge but remains in the pine and oak woods. Through the woods and across U.S. Hwy 259 lie Coon Mountain and Rich Mountain, but during times of heavy foliage they are not visible from the trail. You can hear automobiles at a distance along the highway to the east.

A little beyond four miles into the hike the trail crosses a forest road. A sign points to Red Springs, which lies along the trail ahead. A fairly steep, sometimes rocky hillside marks this section of the trail for about a mile. Beyond the five-mile mark the trail crosses a large rockslide, but it presents no difficulty to hikers. This rockslide resembles a Colorado boulder field, although the rocks are too small to be called boulders.

Beyond the six-mile mark, as the trail nears U.S. Hwy 259, scenic Cedar Creek comes into view. The trail crosses the creek shortly before a short ascent to the finish at the parking lot just off the highway.

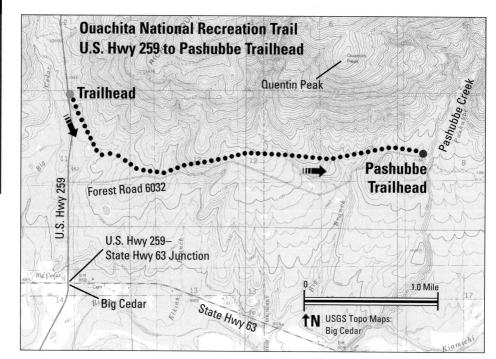

Ouachita National Recreation Trail
U.S. Hwy 259 to Pashubbe Trailhead

Quentin Peak

Quentin Peak

Trailhead

Pashubbe Creek

Pashubbe
Trailhead

Forest Road 6032

U.S. Hwy 259

U.S. Hwy 259–
State Hwy 63 Junction

Big Cedar

0   1.0 Mile

State Hwy 63

↑N USGS Topo Maps:
Big Cedar

❶ U.S. Hwy 259 to Pashubbe Trailhead

LENGTH: 4 miles one way

DIFFICULTY: Easy/moderate

USAGE: Hiking

TH GPS READING: N 34°40.011′ W 94°38.922′

The trailhead is on the east side of U.S. Hwy 259 about one mile north of Big Cedar. A large wooden sign marks the trailhead at the edge of the forest.

Start off to your right down a wide double-track. After a short distance the trail turns left into the woods. Be careful: the double-track continues straight ahead, and you can easily miss this turn. The trail is marked as usual with blue blazes. At about two miles you cross a faint double-track. The trail is well marked ahead.

Keep going eastward, with your eyes on the blue blazes. The next mile or so is a little bit rockier and rougher. Between miles 2 and 3 you cross a gravel road. Again keep going straight ahead. You cross another gravel road just a few hundred yards farther along, and blue blazes mark the trail almost straight across the road. After a short distance you cross yet another road.

After four miles you reach the Pashubbe Trailhead, marked by a parking area. You can get to it from U.S. Hwy 259, as described in the following Pashubbe to Kiamichi River hike.

All in all this is one of the best sections of the Ouachita Trail. The scenic trail is well defined and offers an interesting and not very difficult hike through a mostly pine forest.

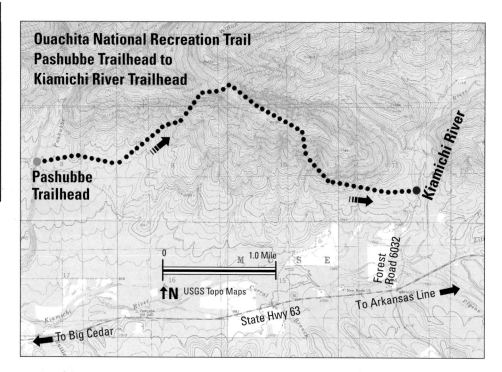

**Ouachita National Recreation Trail
Pashubbe Trailhead to
Kiamichi River Trailhead**

Pashubbe
Trailhead

Kiamichi River

0   1.0 Mile

↑N USGS Topo Maps

Forest Road 6032

State Hwy 63

To Arkansas Line

To Big Cedar

❶ Pashubbe Trailhead to Kiamichi River Trailhead

LENGTH: 5 miles one way

DIFFICULTY: Moderate

USAGE: Hiking

TH GPS READING: N 34°39.610′ W 94°36.089′

From U.S. Hwy 259, a little less than one mile north of Big Cedar, take Forest Road 6032 east for three miles to a parking area. The turnoff from Hwy 259 is clearly indicated by a large wooden sign. From the end of the parking area, the well-marked trail starts out to the east.

This trail is more difficult than the Big Cedar to Pashubbe section, with some rocky areas and fairly steep climbs and descents. This trailhead marks the beginning of the upper Kiamichi River Wilderness Area. A registration box can be found at the start of the trail a few hundred yards from the parking area. Shortly afterward you begin to climb Wilton Mountain. This is a fairly steep climb, up a series of switchbacks for a mile or more of steep and rocky trail. At the top of the trail, a great view opens back into the valley to the south.

Along the top of the ridge you are hiking on rocks. This is the south edge of the wilderness area, and signs on your left define the area for several miles. As you come down from Wilton Mountain, the trail gets better, but the blazes are very, very faint. You have to be careful. Although the trail is easier to see on the ground, few blazes can be found.

The trail ends at the Kiamichi River Trailhead where Forest Road 6032 dead-ends. This hike may be done as an out-and-back route or by way of a car drop.

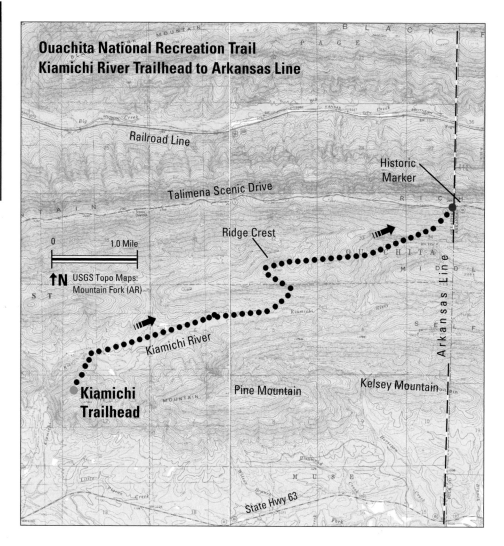

Ouachita National Recreation Trail
Kiamichi River Trailhead to Arkansas Line

Railroad Line

Talimena Scenic Drive

Historic
Marker

Ridge Crest

0   1.0 Mile

↑N USGS Topo Maps:
Mountain Fork (AR)

Kiamichi River

Kiamichi
Trailhead

Pine Mountain

Kelsey Mountain

Arkansas Line

State Hwy 63

➊ Kiamichi River Trailhead to Arkansas Line

LENGTH: 6.7 miles one way

DIFFICULTY: Strenuous

USAGE: Hiking

TH GPS READING: N 34°39.594′ W 94°32.498′

Take State Hwy 63 east from Big Cedar about eight miles to Forest Road 6032, which is on the north side of the highway just past the entrance to the Beech Creek National Scenic and Botanical Area sign on the opposite side. Turn north and follow the road across the Kiamichi River, which might be flowing after rain or a wet period. (If you don't have four-wheel drive, you may want to park on the south side of the river crossing.) A hundred yards or so north of the river crossing a latched metal gate on the right marks the entrance to a dirt roadway. After closing the gate behind you, follow this dirt road about half a mile to the trailhead.

The trail from the sign at the trailhead leads east for hikers going to the Arkansas line. The trail going west from the sign leads to Pashubbe Trailhead.

As you follow the blue blazes eastward, the level trail winds through the pines and oaks of the Ouachita National Forest. A rocky pathway marks the opening section of this clear, well-marked trail, with the Kiamichi River to the south. The trail crosses a number of usually dry creeks in the first few miles, which could create wet footing during the rainy season.

The first few miles are generally east-northeast and level, with an occasional primitive campsite in view. At about 1.5 miles the trail crosses an attractive creek with running water. Plenty of good rocks help to negotiate this crossing.

At about two miles the trail takes a more northerly route, with higher ground visible ahead. The trail stays level until about mile 4, where a dilapidated wooden sign marks the trail. The route begins a long winding climb to the north and up Rich Mountain. This ascent is fairly steep and rocky. It may be hard to follow if the trail is covered with leaves, so you should keep a close eye on the blazes.

A number of switchbacks lead to the ridge at the top, about a half-mile after the ascent begins. The trail levels out for a short way and briefly winds a little to the northwest. Just follow the blazes, which are scarce and occasionally faint through this section. You may need to look backward at times to confirm the trail with blazes for the opposite direction.

Near the top of the ridge you are generally heading northeast, although the trail is a bit circuitous along the ridgeline. At around five miles you start a brief descent. An outcropping of rocks marks the top of the ridgeline, where the trail nearly loops back on itself. It's a good place to take a rest on one of the plentiful flat rocks.

From the ridge you might be able to hear an occasional motorcycle to the north on State Hwy 1, the Talimena Drive. From here it's less than two miles to the finish of this trail section at the Arkansas line.

The descent to the east-northeast is steady and sometimes on difficult terrain. About a half-mile from the finish you'll start a steady ascent on a rough, rocky trail. At about 0.3 mile from the finish you pass a marker on a tree denoting the 46-mile point on the trail. This is the total distance from the Ouachita Trail's beginning in Talimena State Park far to the west.

The rugged uphill ascent to the finish ends at a couple of signs with information about the Ouachita Trail. The highway is just about 20 yards north of these signs, where the Oklahoma-Arkansas state-line signs are posted.

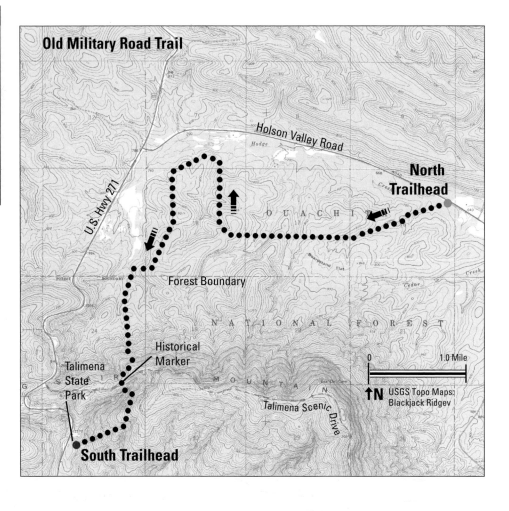

Old Military Road Trail

Holson Valley Road

North Trailhead

OUACHIT

U.S. Hwy 271

Hodge

Forest Boundary

NATIONAL FOREST

Talimena State Park

Historical Marker

MOUNTAIN

Talimena Scenic Drive

South Trailhead

0   1.0 Mile

N USGS Topo Maps:
   Blackjack Ridgev

➋ Old Military Road Trail

LENGTH: 6.5 to 8 miles one way

DIFFICULTY: Moderate

USAGE: Hiking, mountain biking

TH GPS READING: N 34°49.401′ W 94°53.551′

From U.S. Hwy 271 turn east on Holson Valley Road about three miles north of the intersection of State Hwy 1 (Talimena Drive) and U.S. Hwy 271. About three miles east a sign on the south side of the Holson Valley Road marks the Boardstand Trail. Turn south onto the unpaved road, which quickly reaches the trailhead for both the Boardstand Trail and the Old Military Road Trail. Ample parking space can be found near the trailhead.

The Old Military Road Trail is one of the best hiking trails in the state. Well marked and well maintained, the trail leads you through a towering pine forest, up the side of Winding Stair Mountain. It can be done as an out-and-back hike of about 13 miles or point to point, with a car drop at either 6.5 or 8 miles. It can also be made part of a 23-mile backpacking loop by joining the Old Military Trail with the Ouachita Trail and the Boardstand Trail: a rugged two- or three-day adventure.

The trail generally follows the route of the road that was built by the U.S. military in 1832 to connect Fort Smith, Arkansas, to Fort Towson in the old Indian Territory. It is largely single-track, although occasionally you can see the route of the old wagon road.

The trail begins in a southwestwardly direction. At a little less than one mile it intersects with the Boardstand Trail. Proceed straight ahead along the Old Military Road Trail, which is marked with white blazes. After the intersection with the Boardstand Trail, the trees are also marked with yellow blazes, because it is now part of the Indian Nations Trail.

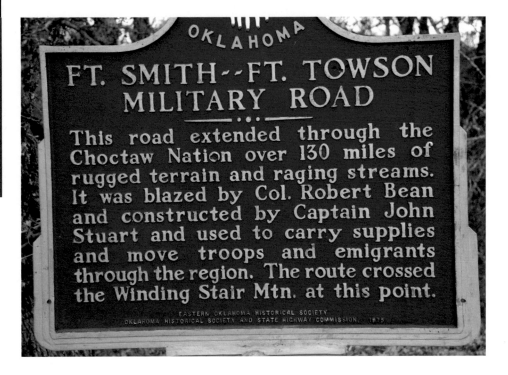

OKLAHOMA

FT. SMITH--FT. TOWSON MILITARY ROAD

This road extended through the Choctaw Nation over 130 miles of rugged terrain and raging streams. It was blazed by Col. Robert Bean and constructed by Captain John Stuart and used to carry supplies and move troops and emigrants through the region. The route crossed the Winding Stair Mtn. at this point.

EASTERN OKLAHOMA HISTORICAL SOCIETY
OKLAHOMA HISTORICAL SOCIETY AND STATE HIGHWAY COMMISSION. 1975

At about two miles you cross a forest road. The trail is well marked and goes straight across the road. After 5.5 miles the Indian Nations Trail breaks off to the left. From here on, only white blazes remain. At this point, according to the sign, you are 1.5 miles from the Ouachita Trail and 2.5 miles from Talimena State Park.

At 6.5 miles you come to the Talimena Drive, a good place to turn around for an out-and-back hike. If you choose to go on, the trailhead on the other side of the Talimena Drive is marked with a wooden sign. You immediately make a steep, rocky descent, then climb in and out of a creek bed and soon reach the Ouachita Trail, which is marked with blue blazes. Turn right toward Talimena State Park. (If you were to go to the left on the Ouachita Trail, you would be proceeding toward Dead Man Gap.) From this point it is one mile to Talimena State Park.

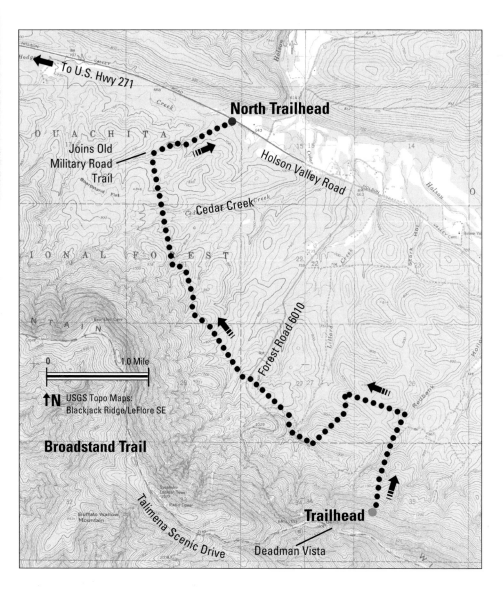

To U.S. Hwy 271

North Trailhead

O U A C H I T A

Joins Old
Military Road
Trail

Holson Valley Road

Cedar Creek Creek

I O N A L   F O R E S T

Forest Road 6010

0   1.0 Mile

N   USGS Topo Maps:
Blackjack Ridge/LeFlore SE

Broadstand Trail

Talimena Scenic Drive

Trailhead

Deadman Vista

❸ Boardstand Trail
South-to-North Route

LENGTH: 8.7 miles one way

DIFFICULTY: Moderate/strenuous

USAGE: Hiking, equestrian

TH GPS READING: N 34°46.339′ W 94°51.421′

The trail starts approximately 10 miles east of U.S. Hwy 271 on State Hwy 1 (Talimena Drive) just past Deadman Gap Scenic Vista. This overlook has no road sign but lies on the north side of the roadway near a sign facing east that announces the Homer Johnston Recreation Area. Park at Deadman Gap Scenic Vista and walk about 0.3 miles east along the Talimena Drive. About 50 yards past a guard-rail look carefully along the north side of the roadway for the blue blazes of the Ouachita Trail. Descend on switchbacks along a rugged, rocky stretch of the Ouachita Trail for about 0.7 mile. Signage indicates the Boardstand Trail (marked by white blazes), which soon joins the Indian Nations Trail (yellow blazes) for several miles.

About 0.3 mile along the Boardstand Trail you can see a barbed-wired fence on the east side. The trail starts off rather rocky and rough, proceeding through the needle pine and oak stands that pervade the Ouachita National Forest. The trail begins to smooth out as it descends slightly in a north-northeasterly route through a somewhat thick pine forest.

At about one mile along the trail you can see a small round pond on the west side of the trail. The broad trail leads to more signage about 1.5 miles along, which indicates the Boardstand Trail and Indian Nations Trail to the left and provides other area information. Following the white blazes of the Boardstand Trail and the yellow blazes of the Indian Nations Trail, you soon cross an unmarked forest service road and the first of many small streams. These narrow streams could make for wet crossings during spring or after a heavy rain.

The trail starts a lengthy climb to the southwest. At the top of the climb the Indian Nations Trail continues to the west, while the Boardstand Trail proceeds west-northwest. (It is unclear whether the Boardstand Trail actually separates from the Indian Nations Trail at this point: the two pathways soon rejoin.) The northwesterly Boardstand blazes become indistinct, and you can see orange blazes for a while. As you follow the trail to the northwest, another small forest pond appears on the left.

After descending downhill, the trail soon heads north, rejoining the yellow blazes of the Indian Nations Trail near one of several small creeks on this stretch of the trail. White blazes soon reappear with the yellow blazes. The broad, rocky trail continues northwesterly, crossing another forest road. The trail narrows and soon crosses Forest Road 6010 at about the halfway mark of the hike.

The clearly marked trail proceeds through a logging area, keeping to a northwesterly route. About 0.3 mile west-northwest of Forest Road 6010, the trail fords another stream and passes a well-made sign pointing the way. Keep a keen watch for the white blazes, as pathways occasionally veer off the Boardstand Trail (possibly the work of hunters).

After proceeding almost straight north, at about 1.2 miles from the finish the trail crosses Cedar Creek, the widest of the many streams along the route. With 0.6 mile to go, the Boardstand Trail joins the Old Military Road, with a sign marking the intersection. The trail veers to the northeast at this point and finishes at the north trailhead parking lot on Holson Valley Road, which leads to U.S. Hwy 271 to the west.

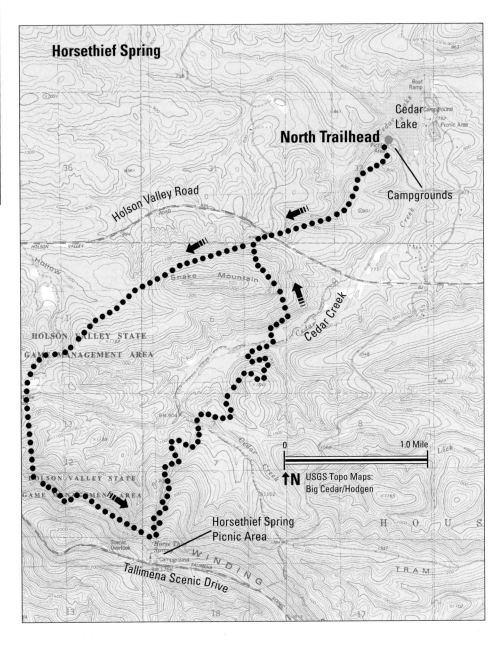

Horsethief Spring

North Trailhead

Cedar Lake

Boat Ramp

Campgrounds

Holson Valley Road

Snake Mountain

Cedar Creek

HOLSON VALLEY STATE
GAME MANAGEMENT AREA

HOLSON VALLEY STATE
GAME MANAGEMENT AREA

Horsethief Spring
Picnic Area

Tallimena Scenic Drive

0   1.0 Mile

↑N   USGS Topo Maps:
     Big Cedar/Hodgen

❹ Horsethief Spring

LENGTH: 12-mile loop

DIFFICULTY: Strenuous

USAGE: Hiking, equestrian

TH GPS READING: N 34°46.660′ W 94°41.565′

The Cedar Lake Recreation area is 10 miles south of Heavener and 2 miles west of U.S. Hwy 59 on Holson Valley Road. The turn off Holson Valley Road is clearly marked. After turning into the recreation area, proceed to the picnic area adjacent to Cedar Lake. A fee is required, which may be paid at a self-service kiosk. The well-marked trailhead is located just west of the kiosk.

This hike can be started in three different locations: at Horsethief Spring picnic ground along State Hwy 1 (Talimena Drive) in the south, on Holson Valley Road, or at Cedar Lake Recreation Area in the north. We recommend starting the hike at Cedar Lake Recreation Area, which has good parking, restrooms, and water. The trailhead is easy to find. The trail loops, and you can return to the same starting point to complete your hike.

The trail is named for Horsethief Spring, atop Winding Stair Mountain. The spring has always provided water, even in dry years, and also furnished a lookout. Thus it became a hideout for horse thieves. The route followed by these outlaws now offers a good hike up and down the side of Winding Stair Mountain.

The trail is marked by white blazes, which you should watch carefully. At some points the trail follows or is intersected by old logging roads. Equestrian trails marked by yellow blazes and yellow numbered signs cross or follow the trail. Ignore the yellow markings and follow the white blazes.

You can obtain a map of the equestrian trails at the visitor center at the intersection of State Hwy 1 and U.S. Hwy 271. This may be useful if you find yourself lost on any of these trails, which are marked by numbers.

After about half a mile you cross a park maintenance road. Be careful to follow the white arrows and look for the white blazes marking the place where the trail resumes several hundred yards to your right on the other side of road. At about one mile you cross Holson Valley Road. The trail proceeds almost straight ahead. You can pick up the white blazes on the other side of the road.

At approximately 1.5 miles the trail forks at a sign. Proceed to the right for a counterclockwise hike. This is a confusing area. A horse trail comes in from the left, and the trail directly to Horsethief Spring via the east fork goes straight ahead. The trail to the right climbs and after a little more than a mile descends into a creek bed. From there you begin to climb to the top of Winding Stair Mountain, ascending over 1,000 feet. The entire trail passes through heavily wooded areas, with tall pines interspersed with other trees such as myrtles, sumacs, red buds, and cottonwoods. Near the top the trail begins to switchback. At about six miles it intersects the Ouachita National Recreation Trail, which is marked by blue blazes.

Turn left (east) and stay on the Ouachita Trail for about one mile to Horsethief Spring. The campground and spring up the hill to your right provide a good spot for a rest. Continue east approximately another quarter-mile, where you again intersect the Horsethief Spring loop, marked by white blazes. A sign here directs you to Cedar Lake. Turn left (north) onto this loop. You are now back on the Horsethief Spring Trail. This leads back to the east-west fork after about four miles. From there retrace your steps to the Cedar Lake Trailhead.

This rewarding hike can also be done as an out-and-back hike. It provides good views to the north and is one of the better trails in the Ouachita National Forest.

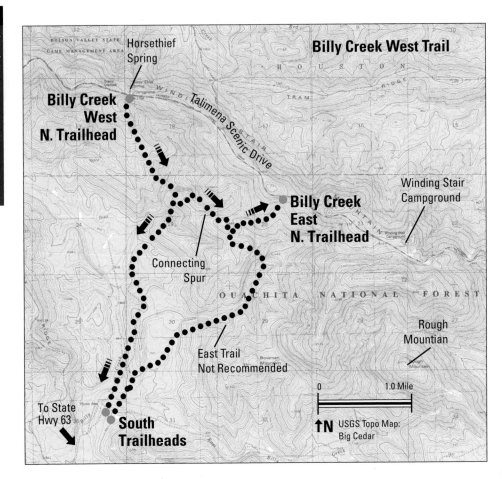

Billy Creek West Trail

Horsethief
Spring

**Billy Creek
West
N. Trailhead**

Talimena Scenic Drive

Winding Stair
Campground

**Billy Creek
East
N. Trailhead**

Connecting
Spur

East Trail
Not Recommended

Rough
Mountain

OUACHITA   NATIONAL   FOREST

0   1.0 Mile

To State
Hwy 63

**South
Trailheads**

↑N   USGS Topo Map:
Big Cedar

❺ Billy Creek West Trail

LENGTH: 10 miles out and back

DIFFICULTY: Moderate

USAGE: Hiking

TH GPS READING: N 34°44.226′ W 94°43.668′

The Horsethief Spring picnic area is approximately five miles west of the intersection of U.S. Hwy 259 and State Hwy 1 (Talimena Drive). The trailhead is on the south side of the road directly across from the west end of the Horsethief Spring picnic area. It is marked only with a sign prohibiting equestrian use. You need to look closely to find the trailhead, but the trail itself is obvious and is marked by white blazes.

The Billy Creek West Trail can be combined with several other trails for a loop hike. This hike is presented as an out-and-back hike because of the uninteresting nature of the Billy Creek East Trail, which is not recommended. The east trail is largely on a road and does not meet any real hiking criteria. Another loop is possible by combining the Billy Creek West Trail, the cutoff trail to the Billy Creek East Trail, and a portion of the Ouachita Trail. This makes a hike of about seven miles, beginning and ending at Horsethief Spring. The Billy Creek West Trail can also be accessed from the Billy Creek Campground on the south, but that requires a short hike on a forest road.

The first part of the Billy Creek West Trail is through new-growth pines in a part of the forest where a fire has occurred in recent times. This area provides a chance to observe how a pine forest rejuvenates itself after a fire as part of nature's cycle. At about two miles you come to an intersection with the cutoff trail that leads to the Billy Creek East Trail. Continue on the Billy Creek West Trail. The sign says that it is 3.1 miles to the Billy Creek Campground.

After about another mile you come to a forest road. Turn to your right and go down the road about 100 yards, picking up the trail again on your left. This is probably the trickiest place on the trail. Look carefully for yellow blazes on the trees to your right and then to your left, as the trail proceeds back off the road into the woods. From this point you cross and recross Forest Road 6020B, and the hike is fairly bland. At five miles you come to a road leading to the Billy Creek East Trail; at this point retrace the trail back to Horsethief Spring.

If you are going to continue to the Billy Creek Campground rather than return to the trailhead, turn right, go about 50 yards, then turn left and follow the forest road to the campground. After a few hundred yards a trail is marked by yellow blazes on your right. Don't take this trail. Continue down the road, crossing two low-water bridges. In less than half a mile you reach the Billy Creek Campground.

❻ Beech Creek National Scenic and Botanical Area

The Beech Creek National Scenic and Botanical Area was established to protect the beech trees that grow in this area, the westernmost point in the United States where they occur. The beech trees scattered through the forest can be recognized by their smooth, silver-gray bark. The hikes in this area are also defined by Beech Creek itself, which runs through the middle of the trail system for about six miles. The creek and its tributaries must be crossed and recrossed on most hikes. The trails were established by the Oklahoma Sierra Club with the help of the U.S. Forest Service.

The good news about the Beech Creek hikes is their remote wilderness setting. This is also the bad news, because the trails are largely unmaintained. Much of the signage has disappeared, and the trails are often overgrown and occasionally blocked by fallen trees.

Fortunately the Beech Creek Trail, the Turkey Snout Loop, and the Walnut Mountain Loop are

well marked by white blazes and for the most part not too difficult to follow. The Turkey Snout Loop and the Beech Creek Trail to the Cascades are the most-used trails and in the best condition. Both offer reasonable day hikes in a pretty setting. The Walnut Mountain Loop is difficult and provides a strenuous adventure.

*The Cascades mark one of the more scenic stretches along
Beech Creek in the untrammeled Beech Creek National
Scenic and Botanical Area.*

❻ Beech Creek Trail to the Cascades

LENGTH: 9 miles out and back

DIFFICULTY: Moderate

USAGE: Hiking

TH GPS READING: N 34°35.785′ W 94°29.977′

The Beech Creek Recreation Area is marked by a large wooden sign on the south side of State Hwy 63, six miles east of the intersection of Hwy 63 and U.S. Hwy 259. Turn south on the graveled Forest Road 6026. At about five miles, unpaved Forest Road K68A is straight ahead. Take this road until it dead-ends at the parking area. The trailhead is at the end of the parking lot, marked by white blazes. This location is also the trailhead for the West Turkey Snout Loop and the Walnut Mountain Loop. The trailhead is on the right just before the earthen mound that blocks Forest Road K68A to the south. You can also access the Beech Creek Trail straight ahead down the now-closed road.

The trail is flat and well marked for the first 1.8 miles. This is also the west branch of the Turkey Snout Loop. Shortly after you cross Beech Creek, you come to a T intersection. This is the Beech Creek Trail. Turn right (southwest) and follow the trail past its intersection with the Walnut Mountain Trail. The trail crosses a tributary of Beech Creek and is then intersected from the right by a spur trail to the Cascades, marked by a post. The Cascades is one of the prettiest spots on Beech Creek and a good place to rest or camp.

Returning by a slightly different route, stay on the Beech Creek Trail past the turnoff to the west branch of the Turkey Snout Trail on which you came out. The Beech Creek Trail widens into an old road, which is largely overgrown. The road is washed out at the Beech Creek crossing, so you need to climb down to the creek to find a place to cross on the rocks. On the other side you have to deal with some brambles to regain the trail, which takes you to a similar creek crossing at Turkey Snout Creek and then back to the trailhead. Just before this creek the east loop of Turkey Snout Trail swings off to the right, making a 1.6-mile loop back to the trailhead.

❻ Turkey Snout Loop

LENGTH: 4.3-mile loop

DIFFICULTY: Easy

USAGE: Hiking

TH GPS READING: N 34°35.785′ W 94°29.977′

See *Beech Creek Trail to the Cascades hike.*

This is a good short hike that combines the west and east legs of the Turkey Snout Loop and part of the Beech Creek Trail. Start in the same manner as for the Beech Creek Trail hike. At the intersection with the Beech Creek Trail at 1.8 miles, turn left. Just before the Turkey Snout Creek crossing, turn right and take the east Turkey Snout Loop back to the trailhead.

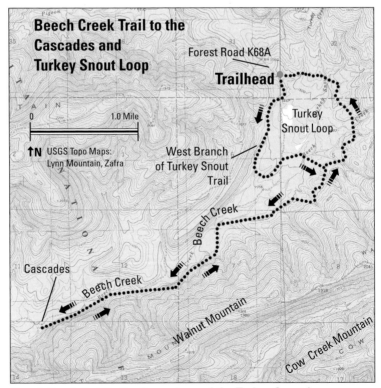

Beech Creek Trail to the Cascades and the Turkey Snout Loop

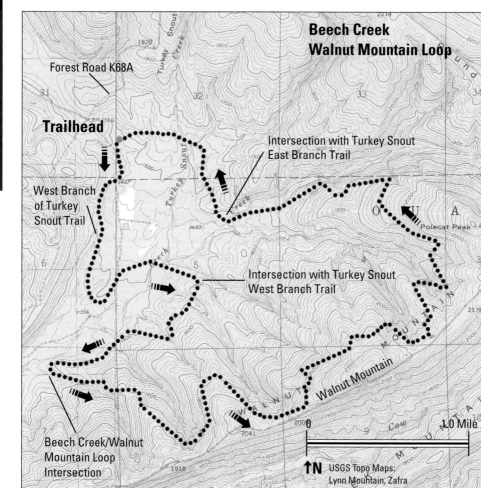

**Beech Creek
Walnut Mountain Loop**

Forest Road K68A

Trailhead

Intersection with Turkey Snout
East Branch Trail

West Branch
of Turkey
Snout Trail

Polecat Peak

Intersection with Turkey Snout
West Branch Trail

Walnut Mountain

Beech Creek/Walnut
Mountain Loop
Intersection

0   1.0 Mile

↑N   USGS Topo Maps:
Lynn Mountain, Zafra

❻ Walnut Mountain Loop

LENGTH: 10.5-mile loop

DIFFICULTY: Strenuous

USAGE: Hiking

SPECIAL NOTE: Trail poorly maintained and difficult in sections

TH GPS READING: N 34°35.785′ W 94°29.977′

See *Beech Creek Trail to the Cascades hike.*

Start in the same manner as for the Beech Creek Trail hike. When you reach the T intersection at 1.8 miles, turn right on the Beech Creek Trail. At about 3.1 miles from the trailhead the Walnut Mountain Trail intersects the Beech Creek Trail on the left. The intersection is marked by a dilapidated, propped-up wooden sign and is fairly obvious. You are above the creek at this point. If you drop back down to creek level, you have gone too far. The Walnut Mountain loop is 6.6 miles long and returns to the Beech Creek Trail farther east.

This loop trail begins with a climb up Walnut Mountain. The trail is not too steep but is poorly maintained. Many downed trees cross the trail, and vines have overgrown sections of the route. Fortunately it is well marked with white blazes. As you cross the top of Walnut Mountain and swing to the east and down the eastern slope, the trail improves. Some good stretches cut through the forest. About a half-mile from the intersection with the Beech Creek Trail is a large stand of the signature American beech trees.

After 6.6 miles of mostly tough, slow hiking, you return to the Beech Creek Trail. You are now about one mile from the trailhead. Turn right and hike back across Beech Creek and Turkey Snout Creek to the trailhead.

This is an adventurous and interesting hike but should only be undertaken if you are committed to some slow going over fallen trees and through occasional bramble patches.

➐ David Boren Hiking Trail

Beavers Bend State Park

The David Boren Hiking Trail is located at the south end of Broken Bow Lake in Beavers Bend State Park, seven miles north of Broken Bow just east of U.S. Hwy 259. The trail runs close to and sometimes overlooks the Mountain Fork River, which flows out of the south end of Broken Bow Lake. This river is known not only for its scenic appearance but also for great trout fishing, particularly in winter, when the water is cold. Both rainbow and brown trout have been stocked in the river, and avid flyfishers migrate here from all over the Southwest.

The David Boren Hiking Trail is a series of shorter trails that can be connected in various ways for hikes of different distances and levels of difficulty: the Beaver Lodge Trail (1 mile), Skyline Trail (5 miles), Cedar Bluff Nature Trail (1 mile), Deer Crossing Trail (2 miles), Lookout Mountain Trail (1.5 miles), Beaver Creek Trail (1 mile), and Southpark Trail (1 mile).

The trail also connects to the mile-long Forest Heritage Tree Trail. The David Boren Hiking Trail is well marked throughout with red blazes on white backgrounds.

The three hikes below can all be done as day hikes, but other combinations are available. With a car drop or some road hiking, it is possible to do the whole trail in one day. No matter what part of the trail system you choose to hike, you are rewarded by some of the best-marked and best-maintained trails in the state. They take you through a beautiful mountain area and are definitely some of Oklahoma's premier hiking venues.

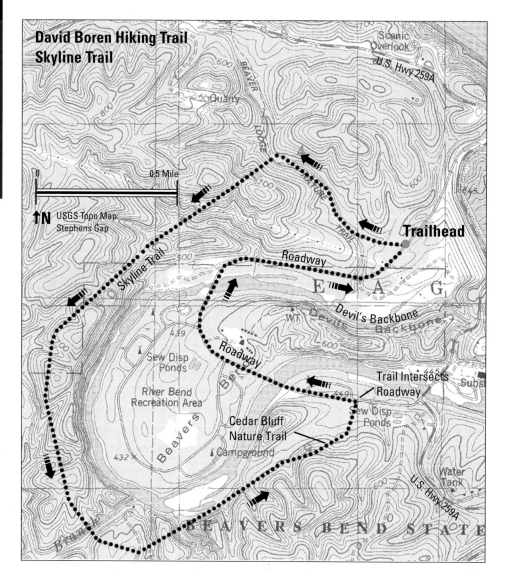

David Boren Hiking Trail
Skyline Trail

Scenic Overlook

U.S. Hwy 259A

Trailhead

0   0.5 Mile

↑N USGS Topo Map:
     Stephens Gap

Quarry

BEAVER LODGE

SKYLINE TRAIL

Skyline Trail

Roadway

E   A   G

Devil's Backbone

Roadway

Sew Disp
Ponds

River Bend
Recreation Area

WT

Devils Backbone

Trail Intersects
Roadway

Subs

Cedar Bluff
Nature Trail

Sew Disp
Ponds

Beavers B

Campground

Water
Tank

U.S. Hwy 259A

BEAVERS BEND STATE

❼ Skyline Trail
Beaver Lodge Trail to Cedar Bluff Nature Trail

LENGTH: 8 miles (6.5 miles of trail plus 1.5 miles on the road to return to the trailhead)

DIFFICULTY: Strenuous

USAGE: Hiking

TH GPS READING: N 34°08.709' W 94°41.412'

From U.S. Hwy 259 take 259A east 3.5 miles to Beavers Bend State Park. Continue one mile to the Forest Heritage Center, where you turn left. When the road dead-ends, turn left again and proceed past the fly shop and the miniature train. The trailhead on your left is marked by a green wooden sign for the Beaver Lodge Trail. The trail starts beyond a gate at the northwest end of the parking lot.

The trail starts down a wide double-track across a bridge over the river. Follow the trail northwest for about half a mile to the trailhead for the Skyline Trail. The trail is well marked. Cross over the wooden bridge on your left and immediately begin a steep uphill climb. At little more than one mile the trail meets a gravel road. After you travel down the gravel road to your right a few hundred yards the trail exits to the left.

At three miles you cross Bee Creek three times: across, back, and then across again. During most of the year you can cross on rocks. When the water flows in the spring you may have to wade. Just on the other side of the last crossing is an extremely steep climb: steps have been constructed in the side of the hill.

After six miles you come to a beautiful overlook and an intersection with the Cedar Bluff Nature Trail, which is on your left. Take this trail to the trailhead on U.S. Hwy 259A. The Cedar Bluff trail is marked with blue blazes. From here turn left and walk 1.5 miles back to the trailhead parking on the road. This walk along the road is a pleasant hike through pretty scenery back across the Mountain Fork River.

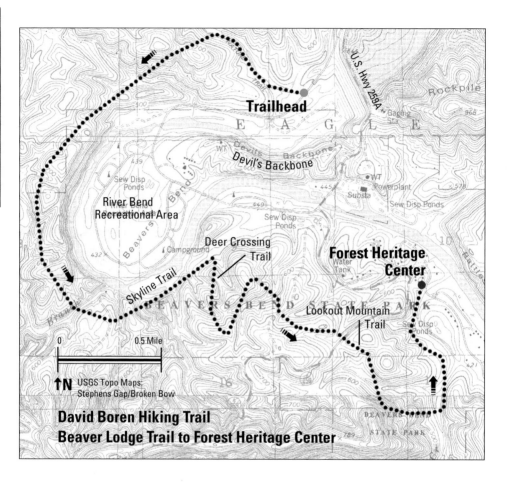

Trailhead

E A G L E

Devil's Backbone

WT

Rockpile

U.S. Hwy 259A

Gaging Sta

968

WT Powerplant

Substa

Sew Disp Ponds

439

Sew Disp Ponds

River Bend Recreational Area

Beavers Bend

445

Deer Crossing Trail

Sew Disp Ponds

Forest Heritage Center

Water Tank

10

Battle

432

Campground

Skyline Trail

B E A V E R S B E N D S T A T E P A R K

Lookout Mountain Trail

Sew Disp Ponds

0   0.5 Mile

↑N USGS Topo Maps: Stephens Bap/Broken Bow

16

600

600

700

BEAVERS

STATE PARK

789

21

David Boren Hiking Trail
Beaver Lodge Trail to Forest Heritage Center

❼ Beaver Lodge Trail to Forest Heritage Center

LENGTH: 10.5 miles one way

DIFFICULTY: Strenuous

USAGE: Hiking

TH GPS READING: N 34°08.709′ W 94°41.412′

See *the Skyline Trail hike.*

For the first part of this trail, see the description of the Skyline Trail hike from the Beaver Lodge Trail to the Cedar Bluff Nature Trail. When you reach the overlook at six miles, stay to your right on the David Boren Hiking Trail, which is marked with red blazes on white backgrounds. You are now on the Deer Crossing Trail.

The Deer Crossing Trail is 1.8 miles long. This is a pleasant route through a pine forest with some ups and downs. One stream must be crossed but is dry for most of the year. After 1.8 miles you cross U.S. Hwy 259A and proceed straight ahead on the Lookout Mountain Trail.

This trail (1.5 miles long) takes you to the top of Lookout Mountain and requires some very strenuous climbing, both up and down. As you reach the end of the trail, you intersect both the Beaver Creek Trail (on your left) and the South Park Trail. Take the Beaver Creek Trail a little over one mile to the Forest Heritage Center.

The Beaver Creek Trail runs into the Forest Heritage Tree Trail, which is a loop trail. You can either proceed straight ahead or loop to your left onto the Forest Heritage Tree Trail. In either case you wind up at the Forest Heritage Center. This hike requires a car drop, unless you want to hike two more miles on the road back to the original trailhead.

David Boren Hiking Trail
Loop Trail from Forest Heritage Center

Forest Heritage Center Trailhead

Water Tank

Beaver Creek Trail

Lookout Mountain Trail

0   0.5 Mile

N USGS Topo Maps:
Stephens Gap/Broken Bow

❼ Loop Trail from Forest Heritage Center

LENGTH: 3-mile loop

DIFFICULTY: Moderate (some steep climbing)

USAGE: Hiking, mountain biking

TH GPS READING: N 34°07.950′ W 94°40.829′

See *the Skyline Trail hike. The trailhead is located behind the woodshed in the parking lot of the Forest Heritage Center.*

This trail is a very good loop trail for a moderate day hike. You begin the hike along the Forest Heritage Tree Trail. At the first Y proceed to your left. After approximately half a mile the trail loops to your right. You can see the Beaver Creek Trail straight ahead.

Continue on the Beaver Creek Trail to its intersection with the Lookout Mountain Trail. Turn right onto the Lookout Mountain Trail. A sign at this point warns of a steep 0.7-mile climb. This warning is well taken: you are in for a steep climb to the top of Lookout Mountain.

From the top of Lookout Mountain you descend to the place where the trail crosses U.S. Hwy 259A. Just before you get to the highway, you come to a well-marked intersection with a trail on your right. This leads you a half-mile to the Forest Heritage Center.

❽ Lakeview Lodge Trail

LENGTH: 4-mile loop

DIFFICULTY: Easy

USAGE: Hiking, mountain biking

TH GPS READING: N 34°10.456′ W 94°43.520′

From U.S. Hwy 259 take Stephens Gap Road east. This turnoff is marked by a large green sign for the Lakeview Lodge. After two miles a sign on your left directs you to the Lakeview Lodge parking lot. The trailhead is located across the parking lot from the lodge, identified by a wooden sign with a map.

This short hike takes you through a pretty pine forest with some scenic views of the lake. The David Boren Trail is much wilder, more challenging, and more scenic, but the Lakeview Lodge Trail provides a fun walk in the woods or a decent mountain-bike ride.

A map at the trailhead identifies the mountain-bike difficulty for the three loops: Loop 1—Novice (4 miles); Loop 2—Intermediate (1.75 miles); and Loop 3—Intermediate (4 miles). The trail also connects to the Indian Nations Trail and combines the three loops for this hike.

Entrance and exit trails are located at the trailhead. Take the entrance trail on your left. The trail parallels the road at the start and then curves to the right in a clockwise direction into tall pine trees, which are typical of Beavers Bend. Although the trail is not blazed, it is easy to follow on the ground. The trail is remarkable for the white quartz rocks strewn throughout the forest.

After less than a quarter-mile you come to a Y. Take the well-marked trail to the left toward the Indian Nations Trail. Shortly you reach another Y. Take the left branch again toward the recreational vehicle (RV) camp. At the next trail intersection proceed straight ahead toward Carson Creek Road. After a little less than two miles, you cross a dirt road and continue straight ahead.

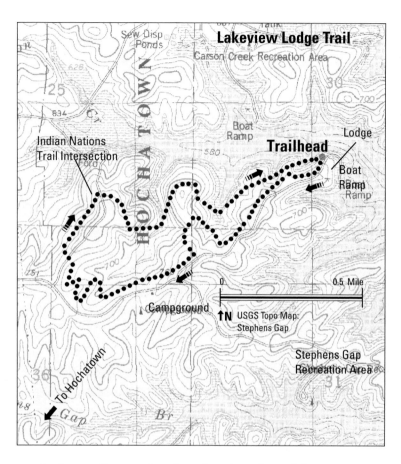

At the next Y proceed to the right, taking the trail that points toward the lodge. Almost immediately you cross the dirt road again. For the next stretch of trail, the lake is on your left. The trail rolls, with no big climbs but some ups and downs. At the next Y continue to your left toward the lodge. This leads you down the intermediate loop and then onto the novice loop back to the trailhead.

The hike can be extended by going out and back on the Indian Nations Trail to Carson Creek Road or by retracing any of the loops.

❾ McGee Creek Natural Scenic Recreation Area

The McGee Creek Natural Scenic Recreation Area (NSRA) is located between Atoka and Antlers. Although part of the McGee Creek State Park, it is separated both geographically and functionally. The state park itself is located on the south shore of McGee Creek Lake and features recreational activities such as swimming, fishing, boating, and picnicking as well as several RV sites.

The NSRA (over 10 miles away at the northeast corner of McGee Creek Lake) is devoted to the preservation of nature and activities such as hiking, off-road biking, trail riding, and wilderness camping. It encompasses 8,900 acres. According to the Oklahoma State Parks and Recreation Department, the NSRA is based on four concepts: (1) a quiet-water zone, (2) a wilderness recreational experience, (3) nonmotorized activities, and (4) preservation of natural and cultural resources. Maintenance is provided by the state park.

Permits are required for the use of the area, but they are free and are available at the office at the entrance to the NSRA. Users can obtain the permits themselves by filling out a form and placing a receipt in a box at the office. Clean, well-maintained restrooms and a picnic area are located near the trailhead. You can also obtain a fairly comprehensive trail map at the permit station. Keep in mind, however, that the map is not really to scale and is somewhat misleading on distances.

More than 20 miles of trails exist in the NSRA, most of which follow the path of old logging roads. Motorized vehicles are not allowed. The wildlife is varied and abundant, which provides an interesting setting for hiking.

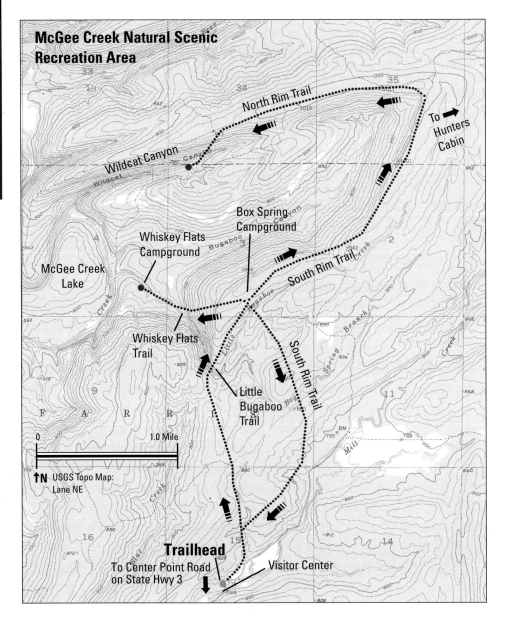

McGee Creek Natural Scenic Recreation Area

North Rim Trail

Wildcat Canyon

To Hunters Cabin

Box Spring Campground

South Rim Trail

Whiskey Flats Campground

McGee Creek Lake

Whiskey Flats Trail

Little Bugaboo Trail

South Rim Trail

0   1.0 Mile

N USGS Topo Map: Lane NE

Trailhead
To Center Point Road on State Hwy 3

Visitor Center

❾ Little Bugaboo to Whiskey Flats to South Rim Trail

LENGTH: 7-mile loop

DIFFICULTY: Moderate

USAGE: Hiking, mountain biking, equestrian

TH GPS READING: N 34°23.359′ W 95°49.515′

The McGee Creek Natural Scenic Recreation Area Trailhead is 13 miles north of State Hwy 3 at the end of Center Point Road. The turnoff from Hwy 3 to Center Point Road is about three miles east of Farris (19 miles east of Atoka, between Atoka and Antlers). The last four or five miles of Center Point Road are very rough but passable. If you are coming from the west, do not turn into McGee Creek State Park on McGee Creek Dam Road. Continue east until you reach Center Point Road. The trailhead is next to the picnic area right behind the office. The dirt parking lot west of Center Point Road across from the trailhead is well marked, with a number of signs.

Begin the hike straight ahead down a double-track that leads into a tall pine forest. Continue on this trail until you reach the Little Bugaboo Trail, which is clearly marked with a yellow metal sign.

The Little Bugaboo Trail is single-track and leads northeast. Almost immediately you cross a creek then come to an intersection with the west branch of the trail. Stay to your right with Little Bugaboo Creek on your right. The trail is well marked with yellow and pinkish-red blazes. After about two miles of hiking from the trailhead you reach Box Spring Campground. Look across the open camping area to your left for the trailhead to the Whiskey Flats Trail.

The Whiskey Flats Trail runs for a little more than one mile to the edge of McGee Creek Lake. It starts downhill and after a short stretch of double-track becomes somewhat rocky and overgrown. The trail continues to be well marked with blazes and is not difficult to follow. It ends at the Whiskey Flats Campground on the shore of McGee Creek

Lake, which at this point is a quiet-water zone. The campground is a good place to rest or eat lunch, with a nice view of the lake. Return on the same trail to Box Spring Campground. The trail requires a fairly steep climb for a short distance, but overall it is not difficult. In the summer this area has a lot of ticks, so do not wear shorts and use plenty of bug spray and sulfur.

At Box Spring are two signs for the South Rim Trail. Take the trail to your right, which leads back to the trailhead. The South Rim Trail on your left heads north and connects to other trails in the NSRA. The trail back to the trailhead is mostly double-track back through the pine forest and easy walking. At Box Spring you have the option of returning on the Little Bugaboo Trail in the opposite direction.

Because of the somewhat remote location, the NSRA trails do not get much use, so the wildlife is plentiful. You may see deer, raccoons, possums, squirrels, hawks, wild turkeys, and a variety of songbirds. This is a good hiking area with well-maintained trails.

Wildcat
Canyon

⑨ Other Hikes from the Box Spring Campground

There are other options for hikes from the Box Spring Campgrounds. Leaving the campground, take the South Rim Trail in a northerly direction. The trail is well marked and continues as mixed double- and single-track, skirting the east side of Bugaboo Canyon. After a little over one mile the trail intersects with the North Rim Trail and the Hunters Cabin Trail.

If you follow the North Rim Trail to your left, after about one mile you come to the Wildcat Canyon Trail on your left. This trail leads down a slight incline into Wildcat Canyon and then to the shore of the McGee Creek Lake. Wildcat Canyon is a pretty spot for wilderness camping. You can also continue on the North Rim Trail for another two miles to McGee Creek.

If you take Hunters Cabin Trail to the northeast, you can also connect to several other trails. In any event, you have to retrace your route to the Box Spring Campground and then return to the trailhead by way of either the Little Bugaboo Trail or the South Rim Trail, as described above.

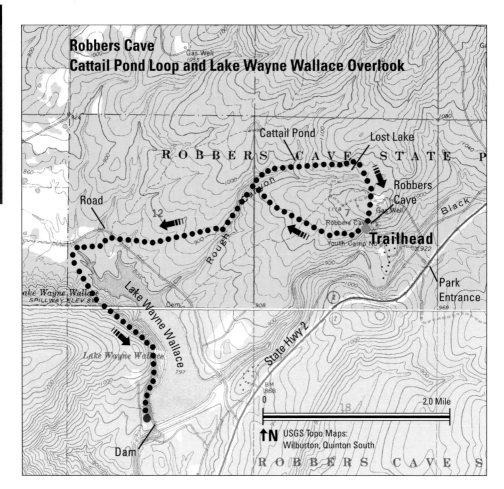

Robbers Cave
Cattail Pond Loop and Lake Wayne Wallace Overlook

⑩ Robbers Cave

Just the name "Robbers Cave" provokes thoughts of Jesse James, Belle
Starr, and the other outlaws who roamed Indian Territory and allegedly
holed up in this remote wilderness. Robbers Cave State Park in the Sans
Bois Mountains of southeastern Oklahoma has no snowy peaks (as falsely
depicted in the film *True Grit*), but it offers some beautiful hiking up and
down rugged ridges and through rocky creek beds.

Both of the hikes start in the Robbers Cave parking lot. First visit
the cave, which is a short, steep walk up the hill to the north. There
you can see where the outlaws corralled their horses and camped in
the cave.

⑩ Cattail Pond Loop

LENGTH: 4-mile loop

DIFFICULTY: Moderate

USAGE: Hiking, mountain biking, equestrian

TH GPS READING: N 35°0.371′ W 95°20.201′

*The entrance to Robbers Cave State Park is on State Hwy 2 about six miles north
of Wilburton. When you turn into the park, take an immediate right and follow
the signs to Robbers Cave. The trailhead at the northwest corner of the paved
Robbers Cave parking lot is well marked.*

To start your hike, return to the parking lot from the cave. The trailhead
leads to the Rough Canyon Trail, which is marked with blue blazes.
Follow the blazes and keep bearing left. You cross a gravel road and
after about 1 mile make a hard right and descend to a creek crossing.
At 1.2 miles you come to an intersection with a trail that takes you to
the right (northeast) to Cattail Pond.

You can follow this trail for a loop hike to Cattail Pond and then
Lost Lake with a return past Robbers Cave and back to the parking lot
(about four miles).

⑩ Lake Wayne Wallace Overlook

LENGTH: 8 miles out and back

DIFFICULTY: Moderate

USAGE: Hiking, mountain biking, equestrian

TH GPS READING: N 35°0.371′ W 95°20.201′

See *Cattail Pond Loop hike.*

For a longer hike, begin with the same route to Cattail Pond (detailed earlier) but at the intersection with the Cattail Pond Trail continue to the left toward the Mountain Trail. At two miles you cross Ash Creek Road. After about a quarter-mile Lake Wayne Wallace is on your left. At this point you begin a climb up to your right through a portion of the trail marked as the Big John Switchbacks. Look for a trail on your left marked by blue blazes. Take this trail, which leads you up to a ridge that runs along the west side of Lake Wayne Wallace.

If you continue up the hill past this trail you reach the Mountain Trail. The hike along this trail provides great views of the lake, the state park, and the entire area. A good place to end this hike is at the highest promontory overlooking the lake, almost parallel with the dam.

To continue beyond this point take the road on your right, which runs to the west. It intersects the Mountain Trail, which goes south past Lake Carlton to a low-water dam near the south end of the park. A number of other trails spread out to the southeast between Lake Wayne Wallace and Lake Carlton and offer other possibilities for investigating this area.

If you turn around at the overlook above the dam, follow the blue blazes back around the end of Lake Wayne Wallace and across Ash Creek Road until you reach the turnoff to Cattail Pond.

Take the trail to Cattail Pond, which is on your left. Although the sign indicates that it is 0.6 mile to Cattail Pond, the trail is rocky and seems a bit longer. Nestled in the woods, the pond is a likely spot for bird watching. It is a good place to rest or have a picnic.

From Cattail Pond continue on the trail toward Lost Lake, which is on your right as you proceed toward the Robbers Cave Trailhead. It eventually intersects the trail that runs down to your left through the rocks above Robbers Cave and then back to the parking lot.

Whether you choose the four-mile loop or the longer hike that continues along the ridge above Lake Wayne Wallace, this is an interesting and enjoyable trail. A number of creek crossings could be wet after heavy rains, but this is still a good hike through varied terrain.

Unfortunately this trail system has not been well maintained. Some of the signage has been knocked down and fallen trees lie across parts of the trail, so pay close attention to the blazes.

Across the highway to the east from the entrance to Robbers Cave State Park is another trail located near Coon Creek Lake. This 1.5-mile loop is designed mainly for off-road biking but is also available for a short hike.

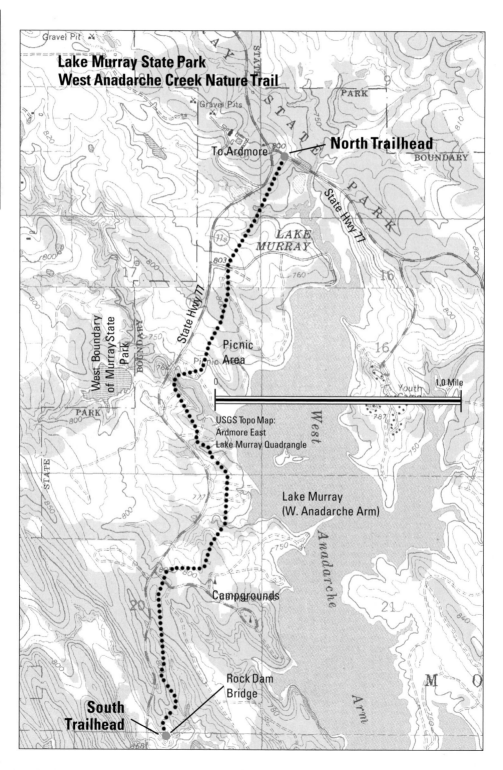

**Lake Murray State Park
West Anadarche Creek Nature Trail**

Gravel Pit

Gravel Pits

PARK

To Ardmore **North Trailhead**

BOUNDARY

LAKE
MURRAY

State Hwy 77

State Hwy 77

West Boundary
of Murray State
Park

BOUNDARY

**Picnic
Area**

Picnic

0   1.0 Mile

USGS Topo Map:
Ardmore East
Lake Murray Quadrangle

West

Youth
Camp

PARK

STATE

Lake Murray
(W. Anadarche Arm)

Anadarche

Campgrounds

Arm

Rock Dam
Bridge

**South
Trailhead**

M O

⑪ Lake Murray State Park
West Anadarche Creek Nature Trail

LENGTH: 8 miles out and back

DIFFICULTY: Easy

USAGE: Hiking, mountain biking

TH GPS READING: N 34°07.969′ W 97°06.395′

The entrance to Lake Murray State Park is located just south of U.S. Hwy 70 about 2.5 miles east of I-35. Follow the signs for the park. As you enter the park a ranger station is on your right. Take the first left. The turn is marked by a wooden sign leading to Group Camps 1, 2, and 3. Just after the turn is a gravel parking lot on your left, with parking for the trail. The trailhead is across the road to the south. It is well marked by a wooden sign identifying the Anadarche Creek Nature Trail.

The West Anadarche Trail System is laid out in a north-south direction between a branch of U.S. Hwy 77-S and the west side of Lake Murray. The trail system covers a total of close to 10 miles from its northern trailhead all the way to Lake Murray State Lodge on the south.

If you live in this area or are vacationing at Lake Murray, the trail is worth hiking, but we do not recommend it as a hiking destination. Although fairly well marked and maintained, it frequently crosses campgrounds or other public areas and in many places runs very close to the road. The area more resembles a parkland than a wilderness experience, and the trail is better suited for off-road biking than for hiking.

Just as you walk into the woods, take the right-hand Y, which is marked with a blue hiker sign. The trail quickly takes you over a substantial bridge. Right after the bridge the trail forks again. Take the right fork.

After a little less than 1.5 miles you come to the Pecan Grove Picnic Area. Keep to your left along the edge of the picnic area and then briefly along an asphalt road. The trail resumes on your left and crosses over an arm of the lake on a stout wooden bridge. The trail periodically crosses parts of the lake on wooden bridges, many of which are Eagle Scout projects of the local Boy Scouts.

When you come to a boat ramp, walk to your right and south across the paved road, where the trail continues. A little farther you encounter a confusing intersection with arrows pointing both left and right. Take the trail to the right.

You next cross the road leading from U.S. Hwy 77-S to the Dukes Forest Campground. From this point it is about one mile to the Rock Dam Bridge. Along this part of the hike the trail gets somewhat rocky and is punctuated by a few ups and downs. Several jumps and ramps have been installed for mountain bikers. The Rock Dam Bridge spans a dam that has created a small waterfall on a creek leading into the lake. The bridge is another substantial structure built by the Boy Scouts. A wooden bench provides a place to rest, eat, or drink. To complete the hike, retrace your route back to the trailhead. If you continue on the trail it eventually joins the Buckhorn Interpretative Trail, which runs to the state lodge.

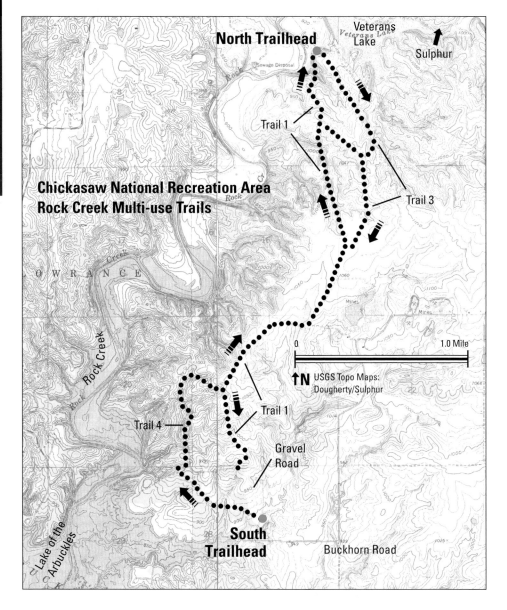

North Trailhead

Veterans Lake

Sulphur

**Chickasaw National Recreation Area
Rock Creek Multi-use Trails**

Trail 1

Trail 3

OWRANGE

Rock Creek

Trail 4

Trail 1

Gravel
Road

0   1.0 Mile

↑N USGS Topo Maps:
Dougherty/Sulphur

**South
Trailhead**

Buckhorn Road

Lake of the Arbuckles

⑫ Chickasaw National Recreation Area
Rock Creek Multi-use Trails

LENGTH: Approximately 8 miles out and back

DIFFICULTY: Moderate/strenuous

USAGE: Hiking, mountain biking, equestrian

TH GPS READING: N 34°26.521′ W 96°59.751′

From I-35 go east on State Hwy 7 to Sulphur. Chickasaw National Recreation Area park headquarters, just off Hwy 7, is a good source for park information and maps. Continue on Hwy 7 a short way after the park headquarters to U.S. Hwy 177 and turn south. Continue south on Hwy 177 about four miles to Cedar Blue Road. Proceed west and south several miles until you come to a gravel road just after entering the park. After turning north on the gravel road, you soon encounter a gate blocking the road and a sign marking Rock Creek Multi-use Trails 1 and 4.

The Rock Creek Multi-use Trails can be a little tricky, so we strongly recommend that you pick up a map at the park headquarters before traversing these trails. Begin hiking up the gravel road from the gate about a quarter-mile and turn to the left on Trail 4. Trail 1 continues north on the gravel road. Trail 4 winds in a westerly direction in deep woods of evergreen and small oak trees. It is well delineated with slat markers. Don't be surprised to see a few riders on horseback anywhere along these multi-use trails.

The Trail 4 pathway begins a more northerly heading about a half-mile from the start, after crossing a couple of usually dry creeks. Less than a mile into the hike the trail comes to a dirt road. Turn to the right on this road, which quickly leads to another dirt road. Go north and a little west on this road until you come to a slender sign for Trail 4, which continues to the right of the road (north). The trail looks as if it gets occasional use by off-road vehicles. Cactus patches crop up frequently along this stretch. At about 1.5 miles the trail reenters heavy woods and becomes a little rocky. Trail 4 soon merges with Trail 1, heading north. Lake of the Arbuckles lies a short distance to the west but is not visible from the trail.

A little past the two-mile mark Trail 1 intersects with Trail 3. Stay to the left on Trail 1, which is generally flat to this point. At about three miles the trail becomes rockier and starts a significant descent. A tower and some structures can be seen in the distance to the north.

The rocky descent continues for about half a mile before crossing a shallow creek and leveling off. Less than four miles along the trail you proceed through an oak grove and come to a ridge on the north past Trail 2. Descending through more oak and red cedar, the trail passes near a tower and deep Rock Creek on the left. Just ahead lies the north end of the trail. A trailhead sign marks this spot by a paved road. Scenic Veterans Lake lies about a third of a mile away on this paved road to the northeast.

Going south from the trailhead on Trail 3 provides some different scenery and about the same mileage. You can see the dam at Veterans Lake along Trail 3 about a quarter-mile from the trailhead. The first part of Trail 3 is fairly open and grassy. At about one mile you reenter deeper woods. The trail begins ascending a little less than two miles south of the north trailhead. Heavy grass marks this stretch of the trail, so watch out for snakes.

At about two miles Trail 3 merges with Trail 1, which leads back to the south trailhead. The last mile of Trail 1 passes by a number of trailers and houses just to the east. The last half-mile is on the gravel road that leads to the south trailhead from Cedar Blue Road (not a pleasant finish).

The Rock Creek Multi-use Trails wind and intersect in a generally north-to-south route. Hikers can choose any combination of these trails to get a good look at the woods and grassy fields of this area.

⓭ Sportsman Lake

LENGTH: 5-mile loop

DIFFICULTY: Easy/moderate

USAGE: Hiking, mountain biking, equestrian

TH GPS READING: N 35°13.197′ W 96°34.170′

From Seminole go four miles east on State Hwy 9 and turn south where a sign directs you to Sportsman Lake. Go two miles south to a sign pointing east (left) to the lake. This sign is a little hard to see, so watch carefully. Take this road about one mile to the lake entrance. The trailhead is at Cove 1, just as you turn into the cove, which has a paved parking lot and restrooms. Trail maps are available at the trailhead. From the parking lot at Cove 1, cross the street and walk on a gravel road toward the main trailhead for Trails 1 and 2. At 50 yards on your left is a trail marked "2, 4, and 5."

Begin your hike on the trails marked "2, 4, and 5." After a short distance Trails 4 and 5 go to the left and Trail 2 to the right. Take Trails 4 and 5, which immediately cross the paved road leading to the lake. The trail is well marked on the other side of the road, where Trail 5 goes to the right and Trail 4 to the left. This hike is designed to follow Trail 4 on the way out and Trail 5 on the return.

Go to the left on Trail 4. At about one mile you reach a sign designated landmark B. Keep to your left. Very soon Trails 4 and 5 split. Continue less than half a mile on Trail 4 to landmark C.

Again take Trail 4, which goes to the left. In some places the trail is somewhat overgrown, but it is marked throughout with yellow blazes. Numerous downed trees intrude on the trail, but they are easy to get around.

Some good views of the lake (on your left) are available between landmarks C and D. After landmark C the trail follows along the edge of the lake, just skirting it in some places. After a little more than one mile you reach landmark D. Trails 4 and 5 again join and veer to the left, where landmark E quickly appears.

If you continue from here the trail exits the trees and runs along the road for a short distance before reentering the forest at the Fish Camp. Landmark E is a good place to turn around. On your return follow Trail 5 back past landmarks D, C, and B and then to the Horse Camp Trailhead.

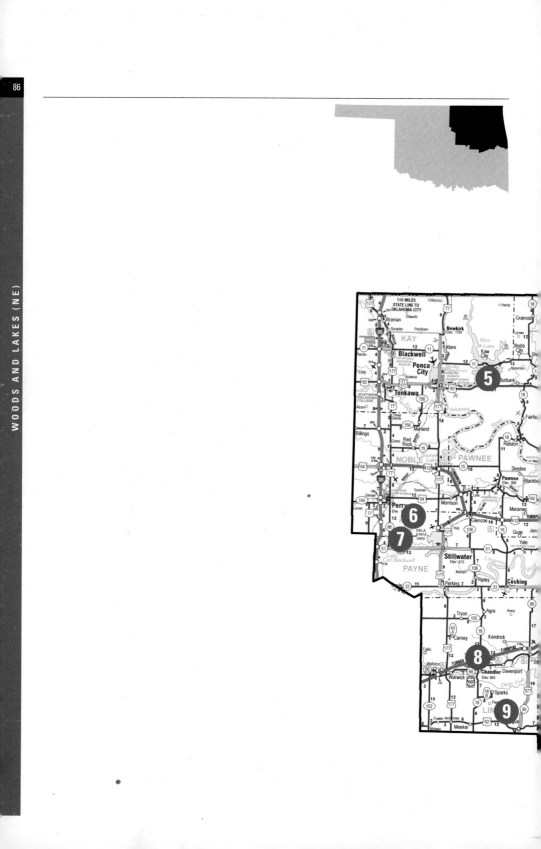

Woods and Lakes

Northeastern Oklahoma

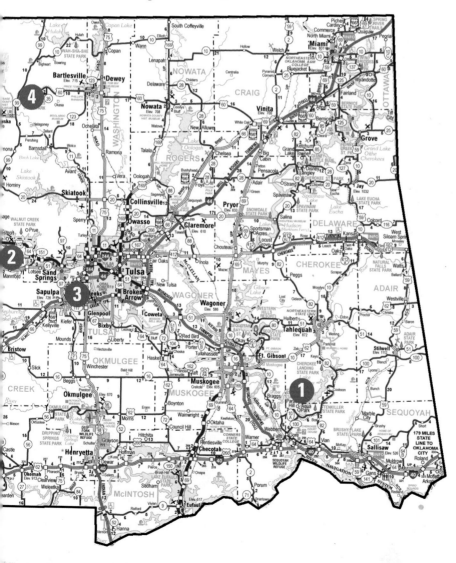

Woods and Lakes
Northeastern Oklahoma

Northeastern Oklahoma is dominated by water. From the mighty
Arkansas River and its series of locks and dams to the many lakes that
dot its wooded terrain, you are never far from some source of water
in this area. This is also where the Big Thicket crosses the state. Made
popular by Washington Irving's account of his travels across Oklahoma,
these dense woods form a perfect background for many memorable
hikes. Most of the hikes in this area are near some body of water and
virtually all are in wooded terrain.

Mountain bikers have been particularly important in the establishment
and maintenance of trails in northeastern Oklahoma. The trails at Lake
McMurtry, Keystone, Turkey Mountain, and Green Leaf can be largely
attributed to the volunteer efforts of mountain-bike clubs and are
enjoyable for both bikers and hikers.

Oklahoma's Native American heritage is also prevalent here.
The presence of the Five Tribes and other Indians is evident, from the
Osage Indian Reservation near Bartlesville to the headquarters of the
Cherokees at Tahlequah, creating a historical backdrop for many hikes.

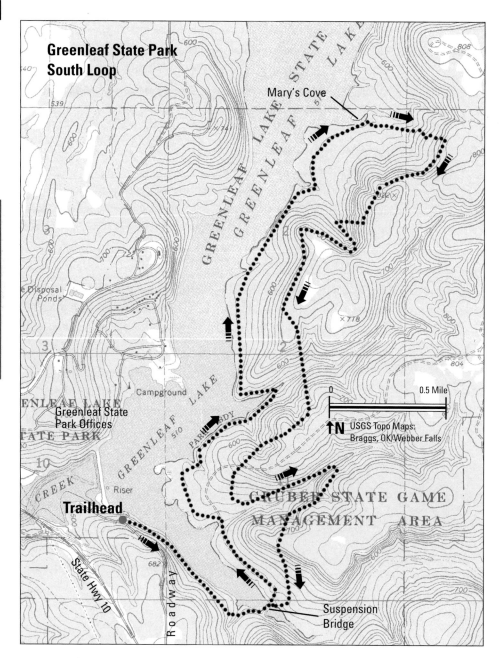

**Greenleaf State Park
South Loop**

Mary's Cove

Greenleaf State Park Offices

Campground

Trailhead

Riser

State Hwy 10

Roadway

Suspension
Bridge

GRUBER STATE GAME
MANAGEMENT AREA

0   0.5 Mile

↑N   USGS Topo Maps:
     Braggs, OK/Webber Falls

❶ Greenleaf State Park
South Loop

LENGTH: 10-mile loop

DIFFICULTY: Moderate/strenuous

USAGE: Hiking, mountain biking

SPECIAL NOTE: No water available; occasional snakes, plentiful chiggers and ticks

TH GPS READING: N 35°36.883′ W 95°10.083′

One of Oklahoma's most scenic hiking trails lies just east of State Hwy 10 between Braggs to the northwest and Gore to the south. The Greenleaf Lake Trail south loop trailhead can be accessed about one mile south of the main entrance to Greenleaf State Park. Exit east from Hwy 10 just south of the Greenleaf Creek Bridge and follow the unmarked rough road north to the south edge of Greenleaf Lake. Park here and look for the blue blazes on the trail leading east through the woods.

Heavily wooded Greenleaf Lake Trail crosses more than 10 miles of secluded, uneven terrain. Although the trail is generally considered part of Greenleaf State Park, much of the route actually lies within the Cherokee Wildlife Management Area. Most of this hiking area is on the east side of Greenleaf Lake, southeast of Greenleaf State Park.

A word of warning: if you traverse these trails in warm weather, be sure to bring lots of bug repellent and powdered sulfur. Lush underbrush, thick woods, and nearby Greenleaf Lake provide a haven for chiggers, ticks, and mosquitoes. Chiggers seem to be the biggest threat. If you explore these woods barelegged and without repellent, expect several dozen chigger bites and about 10 days of itching torment.

Insect bites are a small price to pay, however, for the miles of solitude and occasional glimpses of tranquil Greenleaf Lake through breaks in the heavy woods. The trails are generally well marked, and primitive campsites are available along the way.

Take the trail along the south shoreline about one mile to a suspension bridge. Follow the blue blazes to the left (north) for a clockwise loop, which returns to the suspension bridge from the southeast. It takes more than a casual glance to spot the markers on the trees, but the worn pathway provides a guide along most of the trail.

The west side of the south loop offers several scenic views of the lake. The entire trail cuts through heavy woods and some tall grass. To navigate the 10-mile south loop in a clockwise direction, follow the white blazes eastward at Mary's Cove, which lies about four miles north of the suspension bridge. Watch closely for a small sign and the white blazes marking the cutoff at the cove. The blue blazes north of the cove indicate the north loop of the trail, but they are not well marked and the trail may be difficult to follow. This north loop is not recommended for hikers unfamiliar with the area.

To navigate the south loop, proceed east about half a mile following the white blazes, which may be hard to find at times. Look for blue blazes and turn south on the east side of the loop back to the trailhead. Along the eastern part of this loop you can't see the lake.

The trail zigzags as it nears the south end of the lake and the return to the suspension bridge. Some steep, short grades must be ascended a few miles before the trail loops back to the bridge.

All in all, this trail provides a tranquil and not overly taxing journey through thick woods with occasional postcard views of Greenleaf Lake. But don't forget the bug repellent.

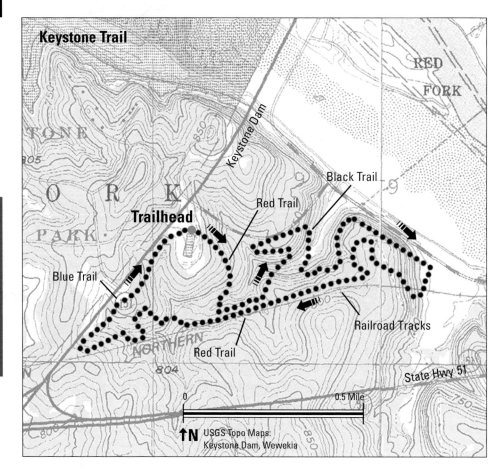

Keystone Trail

RED FORK

Keystone Dam

Black Trail

Red Trail

Trailhead

Blue Trail

Railroad Tracks

Red Trail

NORTHERN

804

State Hwy 51

0   0.5 Mile

↑N USGS Topo Maps:
Keystone Dam, Wewekia

❷ Keystone Trail

LENGTH: 5.8-mile loop

DIFFICULTY: Easy/moderate

USAGE: Hiking, mountain biking

TH GPS READING: N 36°08.345′ W 96°15.589′

The Keystone Trail is located near the Lake Keystone dam, 15 miles west of Tulsa. The trailhead is just north of State Hwy 151, a quarter-mile north of the entrance to Lake Keystone State Park on the east side of Hwy 151, south of U.S. Hwy 64/412. It is marked by a street sign for Old Hwy 51. After turning off Hwy 151 onto Old Hwy 51, make a sharp turn into the gravel parking lot on the right. The trailhead is located to the left, in the southeast corner of the parking lot. The trail begins just beyond the edge of the lagoon.

Lake Keystone (on the Arkansas River) is noted for fishing for striped bass, sand bass, black bass, small-mouth bass, crappie, and catfish. It also has a number of beaches and marinas for water sports. In the winter you can sometimes see bald eagles in the area.

The Keystone Trail is one of many Oklahoma trails that are designed for off-road biking but also make good hiking trails. Maintenance of the trail, which was established in 2002 by the cooperative efforts of the U.S. Army Corps of Engineers and the Oklahoma Tourism and Recreation Department, is coordinated by Keystone State Park with the help of local off-road bikers.

As you begin your hike you have a choice between the Blue Trail and the Red Trail. Take the Red Trail to the left and proceed in a clockwise direction. After about 1.5 miles the Red Trail intersects the Black Trail. Take the Black Trail to your left for a one-mile loop, which comes back to the Red Trail. The Black Trail meanders up and down through a boulder-strewn hillside that provides some short climbs and steep descents as well as a number of interesting rock formations.

At the intersection where you rejoin the Red Trail, proceed to your left, continuing in a clockwise direction. At about three miles you cross an open high-line easement. On the right you have a good view of the Arkansas River below Keystone Dam. The trail is well marked with red and black blazes. Continue on the Red Trail to the point where it joins the Blue Trail. This takes you back to the lagoon and the trailhead.

Overall, this is a good hiking trail. Part of it is very rocky and winds through boulder-strewn areas, but it is easy to follow and fairly well marked. Follow the blazes and do not rely on the signs, many of which have been knocked down or vandalized. The biggest drawback is that parts of the trail are near a road or the railroad tracks. This poses few problems, however, because you do not stay in these areas for long.

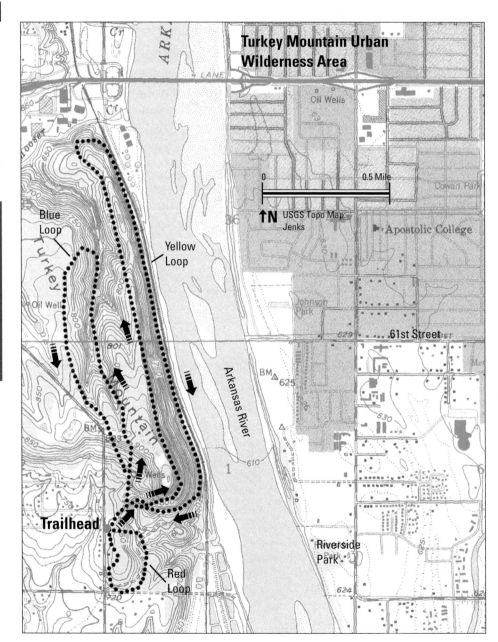

Turkey Mountain Urban
Wilderness Area

Oil Wells

0   0.5 Mile

↑N USGS Topo Map:
     Jenks

Apostolic College

Blue
Loop

Yellow
Loop

Oil Well

Arkansas River

Johnson
Park

61st Street

BM △ 625

Cowan Park

Trailhead

Red
Loop

Riverside
Park

❸ Turkey Mountain Urban Wilderness Area

The Turkey Mountain Urban Wilderness Area is located on Ellwood Drive between 61st Street and 71st Street in Tulsa. Situated on a rocky ridge overlooking the Arkansas River, this heavily wooded area is crisscrossed by over 15 miles of trails. It is one of the premier spots in the state for mountain biking, with rocky ascents and descents and tight turns that require technical biking skills. This is a great place to explore either on a bike or on foot. If you choose, you can simply meander through this maze of trails for hours at a time. For those who are unfamiliar with the trails and the topography, there are three well-marked trails that total about seven miles in length.

At the northwest end of the parking lot just across the paved trail is a trailhead clearly marked by a wooden sign that identifies three color-coded trails: the Yellow or Ridge Trail (five miles), Blue or Pond Trail (two miles), and Red or Lower Trail (one mile). The Yellow Trail actually is somewhat shorter than five miles. Each of these trails is blazed with the appropriate color, with periodic trail markers. Despite the many side trails, in general the color-coded trails are not hard to follow.

Begin your hike straight ahead down the combined Blue and Yellow Trails. You soon come to a place where the Blue Trail proceeds to your left and the Yellow Trail to your right. Take the Yellow Trail, which leads along the top of a ridge for approximately two miles. After you exit the wooded area into an open field, the Yellow Trail turns quickly to the right, back into the woods.

Take the Yellow Trail to your right and pick up the blazes again. This leads you to an interesting hike overlooking the Arkansas River. Although you must pass above a city sewage facility, the scenery is dominated by rocky cliffs that rise on your right to the top of the ridge line and the river on your left. After another two miles of hiking you return to the intersection with the Blue Trail. At this point you can go back to the trailhead or take the Blue Trail.

The Blue Trail ascends a rocky hill and winds around in a northerly direction. After about 1.5 miles you reach a lovely little pond. The trail near the pond may be swarming with hundreds of tiny frogs,

a phenomenon that no doubt provides good eating for turtles, a variety of birds, and other animals. Continuing past the pond, you move out of the trees and hike downhill along a somewhat boring section of the trail that parallels Ellwood back to the trailhead.

The Red or Lower Trail is easily added to your hike and is well worth doing. Walk down the paved asphalt trail toward the river to reach the trail. In less than a quarter-mile the trailhead is on your right. This short but scenic trail winds south and then loops back to the parking lot near an area for horse trailers. The Red Trail also makes a good walk for small children or those who just want a little exercise in a pretty setting.

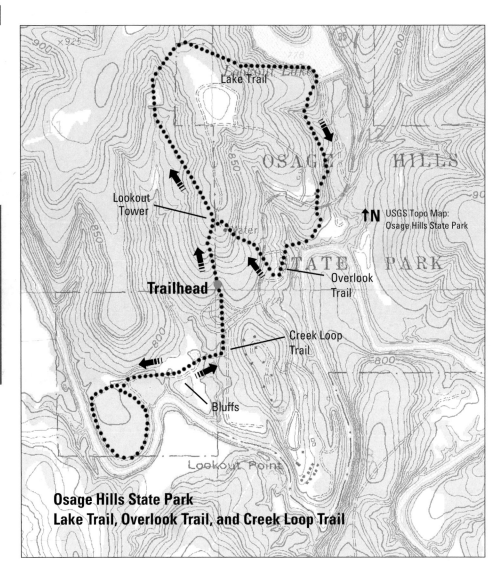

Lake Trail

OSAGE HILLS

↑N USGS Topo Map:
Osage Hills State Park

Lookout
Tower

STATE PARK

Overlook
Trail

Trailhead

Creek Loop
Trail

Bluffs

Lookout Point

Osage Hills State Park
Lake Trail, Overlook Trail, and Creek Loop Trail

❹ Osage Hills State Park

Lake Trail, Overlook Trail, and Creek Loop Trail

LENGTH: 5-mile combined loops

DIFFICULTY: Easy

USAGE: Hiking, mountain biking

TH GPS READING: N 36°44.282′ W 96°11.246′

The entrance to Osage Hills State Park is 11 miles west of Bartlesville on the south side of U.S. Hwy 60. The trailhead is located on the north side of the RV camping area, 2.2 miles south of Hwy 60 (across from RV Pad No. 2). It is marked by a wooden sign and stone steps that lead uphill into the woods.

The trail begins heading north, slightly uphill. At about half a mile the route intersects the Overlook Trail, which proceeds to the right. Stay to your left on the trail and in a short distance you can take a side trail up some stone stairs to the Lookout Tower for a good view of the park.

Return from the Lookout Tower and proceed to your left. You are now on the Lake Trail. This trail is a rocky single-track and is well defined on the ground but has no blazes on the trees. It leads to an open area, an abandoned Civilian Conservation Corps camp, and a water tower. The route is wide and grassy for a short distance after you cross the open area. Then it turns back to a rocky single-track and heads downhill. After about 1.25 miles you come to a bluff above Lake Lookout. A short trail on your left leads down to a parking area and boat ramp near the edge of the lake. If you take this trail, return to the Lake Trail to complete your hike.

After about 2.5 miles from the trailhead you cross a paved road. The trail is well marked on the other side. Just beyond the paved road the trail crosses a rock slab over a creek, with several trails leading away from it. Follow an uphill trail straight ahead all the way back to the Y where the Overlook Trail meets the Lake Trail. Turn left and proceed to the trailhead.

To continue this hike, you cross the RV park to the south. Another well-marked trailhead has a wooden sign for "Hiking Trails." You begin by walking down a dirt road. After about 100 yards take the trail on your right. Soon you come to a sign indicating that the Creek Loop Trail is straight ahead. A trail to the bluffs is on your left.

The well-maintained Creek Loop Trail is the prettiest trail in the park. It is a grassy double-track through a pecan forest. The trail is about a 1.5-mile loop back to the trailhead. Be sure to take the trail to the bluffs before you finish your hike. This leads you to a scenic overlook of Sand Creek. Unfortunately, it also appears to be a hangout for local teenagers, judging from the amount and nature of the trash in the area. After visiting the bluffs, retrace your path back to the RV camp to complete the hike.

Many songbirds frequent the park as well as deer, which are very tame. Overall, this is a pleasant hike. It is probably not worthy of a trip across the state. But if you live in the area it is well worth visiting the park for a hike or trail run.

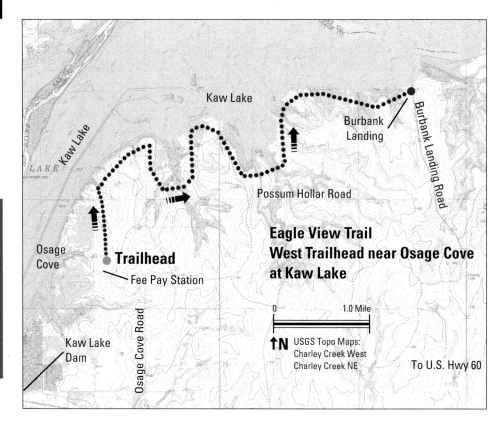

Kaw Lake

Burbank
Landing

Burbank Landing Road

LAKE

Kaw Lake

RIVER

LAKE
ELEVATION 1010

Possum Hollar Road

Osage
Cove

Trailhead

Fee Pay Station

**Eagle View Trail
West Trailhead near Osage Cove
at Kaw Lake**

Osage Cove Road

Kaw Lake
Dam

0   1.0 Mile

↑N USGS Topo Maps:
Charley Creek West
Charley Creek NE

To U.S. Hwy 60

⑤ Eagle View Trail
West Trailhead near Osage Cove at Kaw Lake

LENGTH: Approximately 10 miles one way

DIFFICULTY: Moderate/strenuous

USAGE: Hiking, mountain biking

SPECIAL NOTE: No water available; heavy chigger/tick infestation during warm months

TH GPS READING: N 36°42.849′ W 96°53.719′

To get to the west trailhead from I-35, take U.S. Hwy 60 east about 11 miles and turn north at the road sign to Kaw Lake. After about a half-mile turn right onto Osage Cove Road and drive east and north a mile or so. Kaw Lake, on federal land, was formed from the waters of the Arkansas River. Just before the fee-pay area that leads into the campground, turn right into a parking lot near a sign that marks the trailhead to Eagle View Trail.

Hike north for nearly a mile until you come to a small amphitheater near the south shoreline of Kaw Lake. Turn east on this trail, which eventually leads to Burbank Landing, nearly 10 miles ahead. The Eagle View Trail covers flat terrain through woods and fields, with the lake nearly always in sight. The trail is generally well marked with yellow blazes and yellow slats. You can expect few hazards and little difficulty.

The area is open to deer hunters in the fall, so you may want to plan your hike at other times of the year. During summer heavy vegetation supports an abundant chigger population. Be sure to take preventive measures.

The trail receives light use and may be a bit overgrown in summer, but the yellow blazes are almost always in sight. At the occasional forks in the trail always take the route closest to the water to stay on the main trail. If you lose the trail, just stay close to the shoreline: the pathway will eventually come back into sight.

Occasional wide views of the lake are available through the trees (most striking with reduced leaves and foliage in late fall and winter). At about two miles the trail crosses a small creek and passes through a poorly marked area, but the yellow blazes are rarely far from sight.

A number of rock ledges line the shoreline, providing a good place for a trail break or a picnic. The trail continues for a number of miles through varied terrain but never goes far from the shoreline. Although the lake stays in view, the area farther from the west trailhead receives little attention and few visitors.

Continuing about 10 miles from the west trailhead at Osage Cove, the trail ends at Burbank Landing (just off Burbank Landing Road, which proceeds south to U.S. Hwy 60). This area appears a bit primitive, and the facilities are in disrepair.

❻ Lake McMurtry

Just west of Stillwater, the trail system at Lake McMurtry offers an easily accessible venue for hiking, trail running, and off-road biking. Although traditionally thought of as off-road biking trails, the Lake McMurtry trails are equally popular with hikers and runners, including the Oklahoma State University cross-country and track teams.

The trails (divided into four loops) are on land owned by the City of Stillwater and are maintained by volunteers from the Red Dirt Peddlers, the local bicycle club. The club keeps them in good condition and well marked, including distance markers. Two trails are on the west side of the lake: the Orange Trail (about 7.5 miles) in the northwest and the Blue Trail (about 7.5 miles) in the southwest. Two more trails are found on the east side of the lake: the Yellow Trail (6.2 miles) in the northeast and the Red Trail (6.75 miles) in the southeast. A fee (currently $5) is charged for both hiking and off-road biking, and helmets are required for bikers. The fee can be paid at the ranger station on the west side of the lake or by depositing it into a box at the trailheads in the east.

Each year Lake McMurtry hosts two early spring events: the Lake McMurtry Challenge mountain-bike ride and the Lake McMurtry Trail Run (50 kilometers and 25 kilometers). Participants in the Challenge ride from one to four of the loops during a six-hour time span.

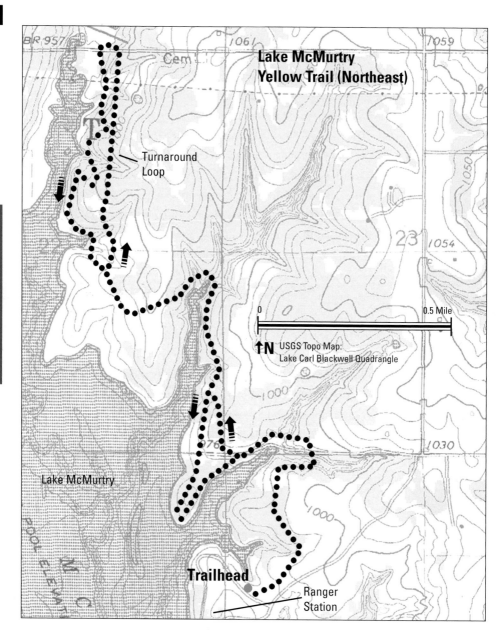

**Lake McMurtry
Yellow Trail (Northeast)**

Turnaround
Loop

0   0.5 Mile

↑N   USGS Topo Map:
Lake Carl Blackwell Quadrangle

Lake McMurtry

Trailhead

Ranger
Station

❻ Yellow Trail
(Northeast)

LENGTH: 6.2-mile loop

DIFFICULTY: Moderate

USAGE: Hiking, mountain biking

TH GPS READING: N 36°11.040′ W 97°10.571′

From State Hwy 51 take Redlands Road north three miles to Airport Road, turn right (east) on a gravel road, and go about one mile to the first stop sign (Cottonwood Road), where you turn left (north). This intersection is marked by an obscure sign for Lake McMurtry. Go north on Cottonwood approximately two miles to a stop sign and Burris Road (a hard-surface road). Turn left (west) on Burris and follow it directly into the park on the east side of the lake. The trailhead is located near a pavilion as you enter the park. You can pay the user fee at the drop box.

The trail starts directly into the woods. Follow the yellow signs. Just before 0.75 mile the trail steeply descends to a creek bed. As you climb out on the other side, you come to an intersection after 0.75 mile where you can go either left or right. You should go to the left to stay on the Yellow Trail. The trail to the right leads across a paved road, which intersects the Red Trail. This trail temporarily detours around the creek bed, which may become a permanent detour and an alternate route for bikers. If you take the detour you add to the hike.

At slightly over 1.25 miles the trail passes very close to the shore of Lake McMurtry, offering good views of the lake and a number of steep climbs in and out of creek beds along the edge of the lake. At just short of two miles you come to a fork where arrows point to the right. If you go to the right in a counterclockwise direction, after two miles you return to the same place, which is identified by the four-mile marker. You then turn right and retrace the original trail back until you come to a fork 1.25 miles from the trailhead.

The trail forks here. Go to the right, following the trail along the lake. This is the prettiest part of the trail, with great views across various parts of the lake on your right. Proceed toward the trailhead until you rejoin the outward-bound trail at 0.75 mile from the finish. From here you retrace your path to the trailhead.

If you want a longer hike you can combine this trail with the Red Trail, about 13 or 14 miles in all.

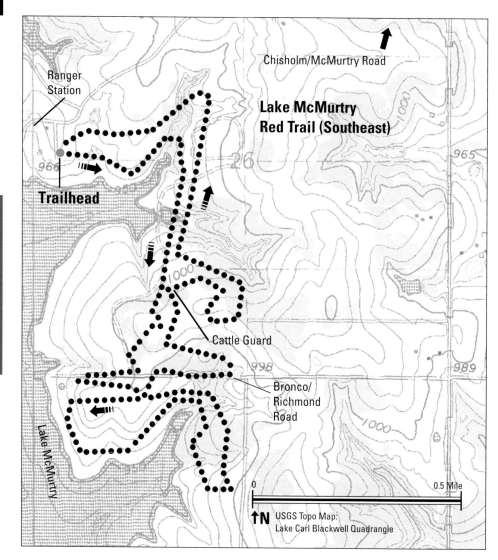

Chisholm/McMurtry Road

Ranger
Station

**Lake McMurtry
Red Trail (Southeast)**

965

966

Trailhead

1000

Cattle Guard

998

989

Bronco/
Richmond
Road

1000

Lake McMurtry

0   0.5 Mile

↑N   USGS Topo Map:
Lake Carl Blackwell Quadrangle

❻ Red Trail
(Southeast)

LENGTH: 6.75-mile loop

DIFFICULTY: Moderate

USAGE: Hiking, mountain biking

TH GPS READING: N 36°10.856′ W 97°10.498′

See *Yellow Trail hike. The start for the Red Trail is located straight ahead on the road on which you enter the park. It is near a pavilion just south of the restroom.*

The trail passes quickly by a small pond on the left and then proceeds along Lake McMurtry, on your right. At just under 1 mile, go over the cattle guard and turn right. After another 0.75 mile cross over two more cattle guards then keep to your right. You are now on the 1.5-mile loop that brings you back to the two cattle guards.

This loop goes across meadows and in and out of stands of cedar trees, offering excellent views of Lake McMurtry. On your return, recross the two cattle guards and continue to the right. After a little more than 4.25 miles turn left on an old dirt road, following the arrow and recrossing the first cattle guard at 4.5 miles. Turn right at this point and follow the trail back to the trailhead.

The trail is just over 6.75 miles, although the trailhead sign says 6.1 miles. The last 2.25 miles include some extremely steep descents, climbing into and out of creek beds. In these areas tree roots and washouts create poor footing. Be careful on these descents and climbs.

This trail provides good views of Lake McMurtry and more varied terrain than the more heavily wooded trails on the west side of the lake.

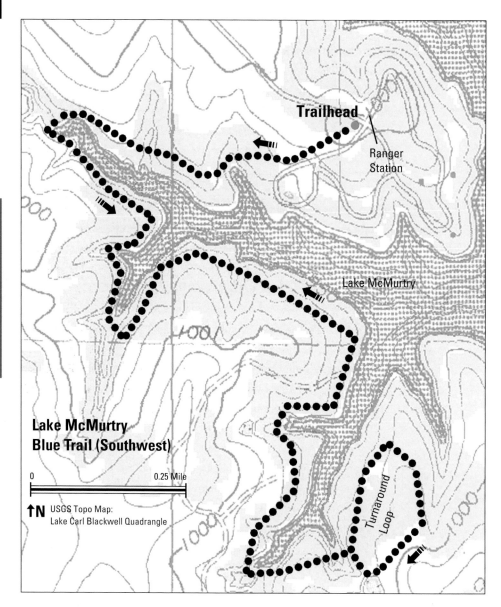

Trailhead

Ranger
Station

Lake McMurtry

**Lake McMurtry
Blue Trail (Southwest)**

0   0.25 Mile

↑N USGS Topo Map:
Lake Carl Blackwell Quadrangle

Turnaround
Loop

❻ Blue Trail
(Southwest)

LENGTH: 7.5 miles out and back

DIFFICULTY: Easy/moderate

USAGE: Hiking, mountain biking

TH GPS READING: N 36°10.260′ W 97°11.351′

From State Hwy 51 take Redlands Road three miles north to Airport Road then turn left (west) on Airport Road. In less than one mile you come to the entrance to the park on the north side of Airport Road. Follow the signs to the west ranger station. The trailhead is located across the street from the station and is clearly marked by a blue sign.

The trail starts through the woods and then briefly crosses an open meadow. At just under 0.75 mile turn left on the paved road, which then crosses a creek. After only a few hundred yards you encounter a well-marked trail to your left on the same side of the road. Take this trail into the woods, which consist mainly of scrub oak trees.

This easily followed single-track winds along the shore of Lake McMurtry, with some good views of the lake. The trail proceeds south with a few ups and downs through mostly dry creek beds. At just over 3.5 miles a half-mile loop brings you back to the same point. From here simply retrace the trail to the trailhead for a total of 7.5 miles. This trail offers a fairly flat hike under a canopy of trees.

WOODS AND LAKES (NE)

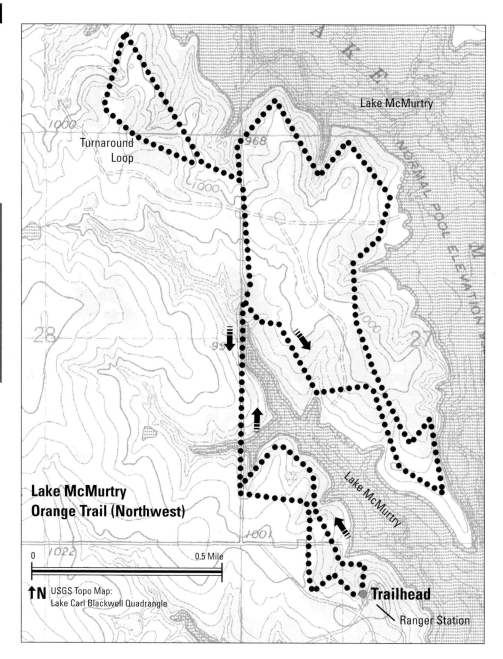

Lake McMurtry

Turnaround
Loop

**Lake McMurtry
Orange Trail (Northwest)**

0   0.5 Mile

N USGS Topo Map:
    Lake Carl Blackwell Quadrangle

Lake McMurtry

Lake McMurtry

Trailhead

Ranger Station

❻ Orange Trail
(Northwest)

LENGTH: 7.5 miles out and back

DIFFICULTY: Moderate

USAGE: Hiking, mountain biking

TH GPS READING: N 36°10.290′ W 97°11.343′

See trailhead directions for the Blue Trail hike. The trailhead is located across the street from the west ranger station and is well marked by an orange sign.

The trail starts through a wooded area for 0.75 mile then leads onto a maintained dirt road turning right (north). If you hear gunshots, don't be alarmed. Two gun ranges lie just off the road, but they are not a problem. At just under one mile you come to a gate, which may be closed. You can pass through an opening to the right side of the gate.

At approximately 1.25 miles you exit the road to the right, passing over a cattle guard. After a short section of single-track the trail intersects a grassy double-track. Turn right and follow the double-track counterclockwise through a rolling meadow dotted with cedar trees. It leads to more single-track in another wooded area.

At 4.75 miles the trail crosses an eroded road and then reaches a cattle guard. Go over this cattle guard and a second cattle guard a short distance later, which leads to a one-mile loop, running counterclockwise through a rugged and less-used area. On this loop the trail is fainter and has some rocky sections. At the end of the loop you recross the two cattle guards and proceed right (south) down the eroded road for a short distance. Return to single-track that leads you back to the maintained road and from here retrace the trail to the trailhead.

The Orange Trail provides a more difficult hike than the Blue Trail, with some short, steep climbs and descents through dry creek beds and a diversity of terrains.

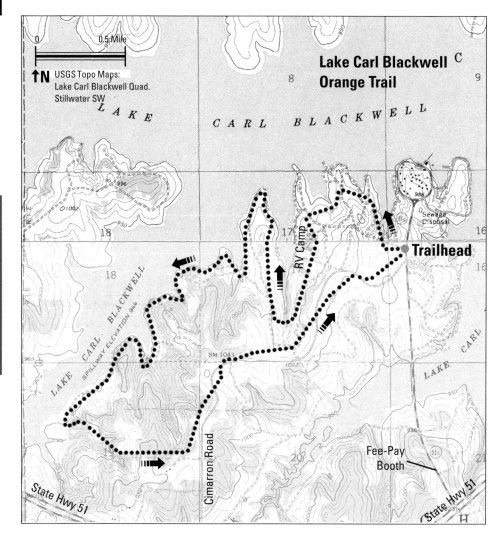

0   0.5 Mile

↑N USGS Topo Maps:
Lake Carl Blackwell Quad.
Stillwater SW

L A K E

C A R L   B L A C K W E L L

Lake Carl Blackwell C

Orange Trail

8

9

996

1002

950

18

17

16

RV Camp

Sewage Disposal

Trailhead

51c

16

18

LAKE CARL BLACKWELL

SPILLWAY ELEVATION 944

960

BM 1043

1012

950

LAKE CARL

950

996

20

Fee-Pay Booth

51c

51c

Cimarron Road

State Hwy 51

State Hwy 51

H

➐ Lake Carl Blackwell
Orange Trail

LENGTH: 7.7-mile loop

DIFFICULTY: Moderate/strenuous

USAGE: Equestrian, hiking, mountain biking

SPECIAL NOTE: No water available; heavy chigger/tick infestation during warm months

TH GPS READING: N 36°07.433′ W 97°12.533′

Turn north off State Hwy 51, eight miles east of I-35 at the sign on the north side of the highway marking the road to Lake Carl Blackwell. Follow the road north past the fee-pay booth a few miles and look for the sign marking the trails on the east side of the roadway. Parking is available in a large lot on the east side of the road, but the trailhead entrance is on the west side. A large detailed map of the various trails can be found on a sign in the parking lot.

Developed primarily as an equestrian venue, the trails at Lake Carl Blackwell also serve well for hiking or mountain biking. The trails meander around a large peninsula of land surrounded by the lake on the east, west, and north.

The Yellow, Blue and Orange Trails have a common trailhead, but the Orange Trail works its way farther north and skirts the shores of Lake Carl Blackwell for several miles. The trail quickly forks to the north on an unmarked exit toward the lake then goes straight north for a short distance before making a loop past a developed area with RV hookups.

The trail is well marked with orange-topped narrow poles and orange plastic strips tied to tree limbs. The mostly flat pathway passes through oak stands and grasslands in a large counterclockwise arc near the lake shoreline. The Orange Trail intersects the Blue Trail and Yellow Trail several times over its course.

After passing by the developed area, the trail sweeps north, coming within yards of the shoreline. From about mile 1 to mile 4 it stays close to the waterline. During the summer the vegetation grows waist-high in places along this part of the route.

After the trail bends eastward past its westernmost point at about the four-mile mark, it crosses some heavily wooded areas, with occasional ups and downs. Continuing back to the east, the trail parallels a barbed-wire fence along the area's southwest boundary. Head north at about the five-mile mark. A large water trough at about six miles marks an intersection of all the trails.

Veering northeast, the hike overlaps a dirt road for a short way before suddenly diverting left (north) off the roadway and into the woods about half a mile from the finish. Watch closely, because this turn is not well marked.

The Yellow and Blue Trails cover much of the same terrain as the Orange Trail and offer a similarly pleasant hiking experience.

❽ Bell Cow Lake

Flat Rock Trail from Horse Camp to Point F

LENGTH: 7.4 miles out and back

DIFFICULTY: Easy

USAGE: Equestrian, hiking, biking

TH GPS READING: N 35°43.782′ W 96°56.344′

The trailhead is located at the Horse Camp in Area C at Bell Cow Lake. From the Turner Turnpike (I-44) take the Chandler exit and then turn north on State Hwy 18. Go about a half-mile to a sign directing you to the left (west) on a blacktop road to Chandler Lake. Do not turn north where the main road turns to the right. Continue straight ahead to Area C. The trailhead is well marked with a wooden sign.

Two equestrian trails are available at Bell Cow Lake: the Flat Rock Trail (6.2 miles) and the Red Bud Trail (11 miles). Both are out-and-back trails; they do not connect. Primarily used by horses, the trails can be churned up and muddy after a rain.

The Flat Rock Trail begins at the west side of the Horse Camp area. The trail generally stays flat and is easy to follow, marked with orange ribbons and occasionally an orange-and-white sign post. After less than a half-mile you come to a surfaced road. Turn right, cross a creek, and then turn right again back onto the trail.

After about another mile the trail crosses the road again. Turn right toward the lake then left through a well-marked gate. From here the trail winds along the lake until you reach another road. This is the turn-around point for this hike, although the trail goes on for another 2.5 miles if you wish to continue.

Throughout the hike the trail separates and rejoins itself but is usually marked with orange ribbons and is easy to follow.

These trails are not highly recommended but are close enough to Oklahoma City and Tulsa to offer an enjoyable hike through mostly wooded terrain.

❾ Prague Lake

LENGTH: 8-mile loop

DIFFICULTY: Easy/moderate

USAGE: Equestrian, hiking, mountain biking

TH GPS READING: N 35°31.263′ W 96°43.348′

From Prague go three miles west on U.S. Hwy 62, turn north and drive two miles, and then turn right (east) and go less than a mile. Signs direct you to the lake at each turn. The entrance to the lake is on your left. Restrooms and a paved parking lot are just inside the entrance. Park hours are 5 A.M. to 10 P.M. The trailhead is located at the southeast corner of the parking lot. It is well marked, with a large wooden entrance and a number of signs.

Although essentially an equestrian trail, this trail is also available for hiking or off-road biking. No motorized vehicles are allowed, although it appears to have been designed for ATVs. The main trail around the lake is marked with pink ribbons tied on the trees. A number of side trails marked with blue ribbons veer off and then merge back into the main trail. Keep following periodic hand-lettered signs directing you to the dam.

The trail starts down an old road that leads to your right. After about two miles the trail narrows and winds through the woods. It is essentially flat, with some steep descents and climbs leading in and out of creek beds. In many places the trail divides. Look closely for the pink ribbons, which are often faded.

At about six miles you can see an open picnic area with an old-time water pump, tables, benches, and trash cans. The dam lies ahead of you. Cross the top of the dam and turn left. A trail goes to the right below the dam, but the main trail crosses the top of the dam, turns left, and leads back into the woods. The trail ends at the paved road to the lake. Turn left and walk a few hundred yards up the road to the parking lot. Additional trails across the road wind through 40 acres of wooded land.

The trail does not have much of a wilderness feel and suffers from the usual drawbacks of equestrian trails: loose sand, horse droppings, and horse flies. But it still offers a pleasant hike or run through the woods around a pretty lake.

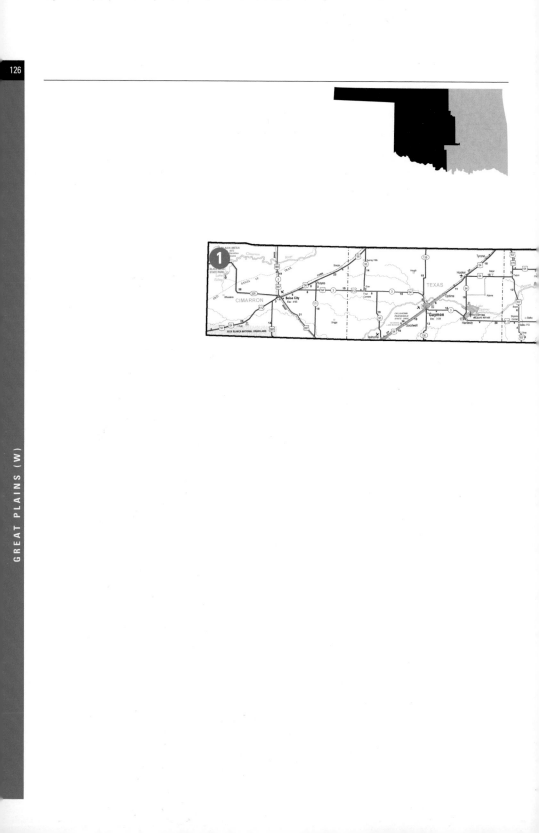

Great Plains
Western Oklahoma

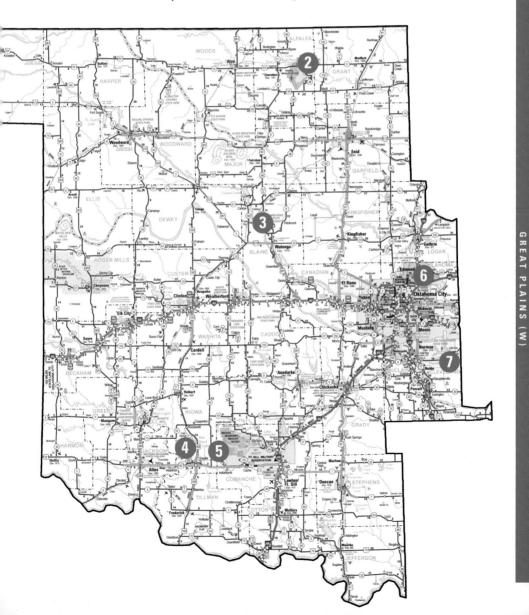

Great Plains
Western Oklahoma

The Great Plains seem to go on forever, rolling away to the west across short-grass country to the mesas and buttes of northwestern Oklahoma and the rocky Wichita Mountains in the southwest. This is cowboy country, where the Chisholm Trail and the Santa Fe Trail crossed the state and cattle still run. Canyons and arroyos are dotted by a variety of mesquite, cactus, and small hardy trees.

While the terrain may be harsh in some respects, it provides a diverse setting. Hikes like Charons Garden and Dog Run Hollow explore the boulder fields and grasslands of the Wichitas. The trails at Roman Nose lead through canyons with a desert feel, and the Great Salt Plains offer a unique backdrop with thousands of birds. Black Mesa, Oklahoma's highest point, is a unique experience, more like New Mexico than Oklahoma. All of these hikes display the Great Plains as a vast and sprawling stage reminiscent of the Old West and Oklahoma's Native American heritage.

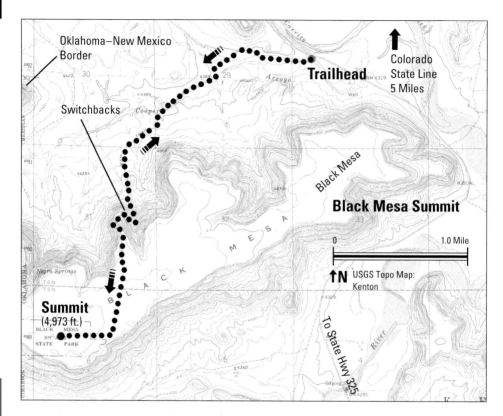

Oklahoma–New Mexico Border

Trailhead

Colorado State Line 5 Miles

Switchbacks

Black Mesa

Black Mesa Summit

Summit
(4,973 ft.)

0   1.0 Mile

↑N   USGS Topo Map: Kenton

To State Hwy 325

❶ Black Mesa Summit

LENGTH: 8.4 miles out and back

DIFFICULTY: Moderate/strenuous

USAGE: Hiking, mountain biking

SPECIAL NOTE: No water available; poisonous snakes frequent the area from spring until fall

TH GPS READING: N 36°57.633′ W 102°57.817′

From Boise City (in the extreme western end of the Oklahoma Panhandle) take State Hwy 325 west for about 18 miles and then north for another 10 miles, passing the entrance to the Black Mesa State Park. Stay on Hwy 325 as it bends sharply to the west toward Kenton. Just before reaching Kenton, turn right (north) at the sign directing visitors to the Black Mesa Summit. The road leads toward the mesa and curves around its eastern end. About five miles along this route turn left into the gravel parking lot for the Black Mesa Nature Preserve and trailhead for the Black Mesa Summit.

The highest point in Oklahoma, 4,973-foot Black Mesa Summit, lies at the end of a delightful 4.2-mile trek across landscape unknown in other parts of the state. Here at the northwestern tip of the Oklahoma Panhandle short-grass prairie meets the foothills of the Rocky Mountains. Rugged cholla cacti, juniper, and scrub oak dot the area's rocky buttes and mesas. Some 600 feet above the surrounding terrain, the entire Black Mesa extends north and west from the tip of the Panhandle 40 miles or more into New Mexico and Colorado.

The well-marked trailhead has several signs with descriptive information on the summit trail and the area's flora and fauna. A rutted jeep trail proceeds west from the trailhead, with Black Mesa to the southwest. The trail stays relatively flat for the first couple of miles.

As the trail meanders west-southwest, the small buttes to the north and the mesa to the south provide great views. After less than a mile you can see a railroad car in the distance to the west. The first trail marker soon comes into view: a green metal arrow pointing the way.

GREAT PLAINS (W)

The third trail marker informs hikers that the summit lies 2.6 miles ahead. The trail makes a sharp turn to the south at 2.2 miles from the summit, and you can faintly see the trail ahead winding up a projection of Black Mesa. The footing becomes a bit sportier along this rocky stretch, followed by the 600-foot ascent along the switchbacks. The climbing gets steep as another trail marker announces the summit 1.8 miles ahead.

While still ascending and a little more than a mile from the finish, you encounter a barbed-wire fence and overhead wire. This marks the end of the ascent and the start of the approximately one-mile panoramic walk atop Black Mesa to the summit marker.

The trail proceeds generally to the south-southeast and then bends to the west. Several yellow signs guide the way. About a quarter-mile from the finish a granite obelisk comes into view, jutting up from the surrounding flat terrain. New Mexico lies a few hundred yards west of this marker, and a small mountain rises far on the western horizon. Less than five miles to the north, you can see rugged terrain and hills in southeastern Colorado.

❷ Great Salt Plains State Park
Eagle Roost Nature Trail

LENGTH: 1.3-mile loop

DIFFICULTY: Easy

USAGE: Hiking

TH GPS READING: N 36°47.167′ W 98°10.951′

Take U.S. Hwy 81 north from Enid to U.S. Hwy 64 and then west to Jet. Go north from Jet on State Hwy 38 to the north side of Great Salt Plains Lake. You might want to stop at the park offices on the southeast end of Great Salt Plains Lake for maps and brochures of the sites. Go a short way past the small town of Nescatunga and turn off Hwy 38 to the Eagle Roost Nature Trail. Information and parking spaces are available at the trailhead.

Although it is not much of a hike, Eagle Roost Nature Trail offers lovely and unusual scenery for this part of the state. The path around this short loop is broad, smooth, and well marked. If you want a little more exercise than the 1.3-mile loop affords, reverse your route and see these views from another direction. You'll probably be glad you did: this is eye-popping scenery.

The trail immediately enters the woods as you begin a counterclockwise route. You can view a wide variety of trees, shrubs, and grasses from the trail. Identification signs for some of the plant species are scattered along the way.

The trail skirts along Eagle Roost Pond and Sand Creek Bay, and the scenery looks more like a southern Louisiana bayou than western Oklahoma. Puterbaugh Marsh appears almost surreal for these parts. Turtles, frogs, and snakes can often be seen sunning themselves on logs in the pond. Sand Creek Bay offers views of wading birds in the summer and ducks, geese, and cranes in the fall and winter.

If you want a little more hiking, go back just past the small town of Nescatunga on State Hwy 38 for the George Sibley Trail. Horse enthusiasts often use this trail, which has a few confusing interior loops that you may want to skip. Bear east a couple of miles and cross the highway to the south for a short walk to the camping and picnic areas around the dam. This is not a well-defined trail, so make sure you have an area map.

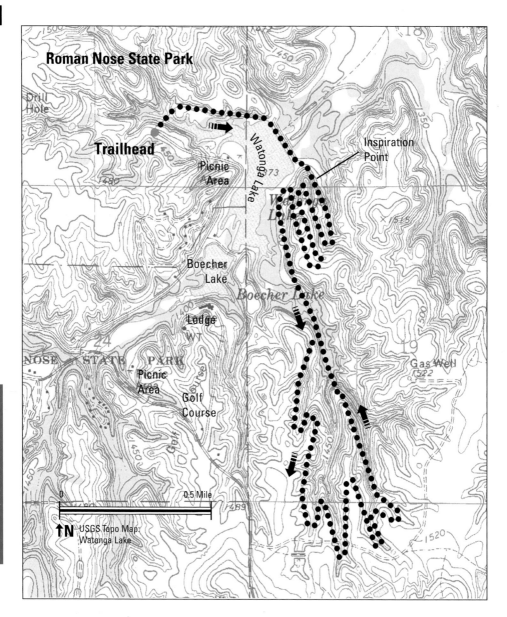

Roman Nose State Park

Drill
Hole

Trailhead

Picnic
Area

Watonga Lake

Watonga
Lake

Inspiration
Point

Boecher
Lake

Boecher Lake

Lodge
WT

NOSE STATE PARK
Picnic
Area

Golf
Course

Golf
Course

Gas Well
1522

0   0.5 Mile

↑N USGS Topo Map:
Watonga Lake

❸ Roman Nose State Park

LENGTH: 6.5-mile loop

DIFFICULTY: Easy/moderate

USAGE: Hiking, mountain biking

TH GPS READING: N 35°56.594′ W 98°25.529′

To reach Roman Nose State Park, take State Hwy 8 north from Watonga a little more than three miles and turn left down a road that takes you straight into the park. A fairly small sign identifies the turn for the park, but a larger sign directs you to Watonga Lake. The trailhead lies 1.6 miles from the Roman Nose State Park gate at the end of the paved road to the north of the General Store. It is marked by an iron gate, which is usually closed. No sign marks the trailhead, so just step around the gate and start up an old road.

Roman Nose State Park is named for Chief Henry Roman Nose, a leader of the Southern Cheyenne Tribe who wintered in a teepee in Roman Nose Canyon from 1887 until his death in 1917. Chief Roman Nose's campground was situated in what is now the state's smallest state park with a lodge (540 acres). The park contains about eight miles of hiking and biking trails.

The park's geological past is as interesting as its Native American history. Chemical sediments left from evaporating seawater covering western Oklahoma produced the park's unique outcroppings of gypsum. These milky white outcroppings are scattered above, below, and along the trails, interspersed with red clay bluffs and stands of blackjacks, red cedars, chestnuts, and cottonwoods. The cottonwoods (an ideal source of poles for teepees) and the plentiful water attracted the Cheyennes to the canyon.

The hiking and biking trail provides a uniquely western Oklahoma experience. Much of the trail wanders along and through mesas and canyons, marked by rocky outcroppings and bordered by cactus plants, giving it an almost desert feel in some places. Although the trail can be

a bit confusing, you are in no danger of getting lost. If you are a novice hiker and want to proceed beyond a walk in the park, this is a good trail to break in your hiking legs. It has a few short steep climbs and overall conveys the feeling of being out in the country.

The trail starts just beyond an iron gate and goes up an old road to the dam across the north end of Watonga Lake. After walking across the dam and making a short climb, you come to a Y. Follow the left fork as it curves around the east side of the mesa. The trail then turns north and leads to the top of the mesa and Inspiration Point. This promontory overlooking the lake and the park provides a panoramic view of the entire area.

From here take the well-defined trail leading to the south. This trail runs down the west side of the mesa to the lakeshore trail. Turn left (south) along the lakeshore trail. At about two miles from the trailhead you cross a wooden bridge over a creek and soon see another bridge on your right. Do not cross this bridge: stay left. This leads you to a series of switchbacks up and down the side of a pretty canyon. Continue to keep to your left, circling the canyon.

After almost five miles you come to another Y. The left-fork trail goes to the lodge. Take the right fork, which leads back across a bridge to the lakeshore trail. Turn left (north), staying to the left and following the trail back to the trailhead.

Minor pathways loop off the main trail, and this hike has many variations. They all offer a generally interesting hike with terrain different from that of the central or eastern parts of the state.

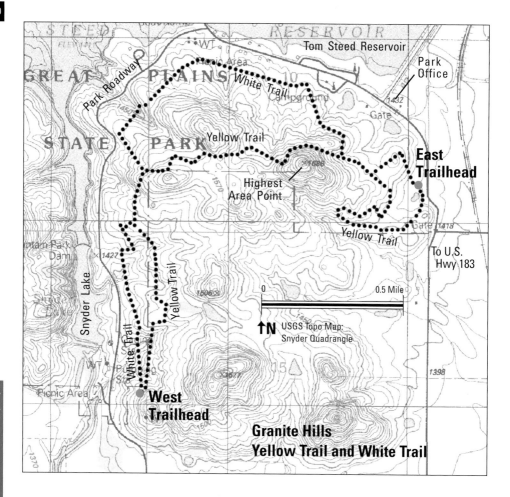

West
Trailhead

East
Trailhead

Highest
Area Point

Tom Steed Reservoir

Park
Office

Granite Hills
Yellow Trail and White Trail

❹ Granite Hills
Yellow Trail and White Trail

LENGTH: 8-mile loop

DIFFICULTY: Moderate/strenuous

USAGE: Mountain biking and hiking

SPECIAL NOTE: No water available; poisonous snakes frequent the area from spring until fall

TH GPS READING: N 34°44.393′ W 98°57.945′

About three miles north of Mountain Park turn west off U.S. Hwy 183 and drive to the east entrance of Great Plains State Park. Signage for the East Area trailhead can be seen from the road as it bends north toward the park headquarters. The sign marking this east trailhead shows a detailed map of the trails in this system, including the distances. Several other signs at the wide entrance to the trail describe the area's flora and fauna.

The Granite Hills Trail System winds around the rugged hills just south of Tom Steed Reservoir in Great Plains State Park. The Yellow Trail begins a west-southwest route past a small pond through mostly tall grass. About a half-mile northwest you can see the summit of a 1,886-foot rocky hill. This is the highest point in the trail system.

The first mile of the Yellow Trail takes a circuitous clockwise route. Occasional yellow markers indicate the trail. These markers have been installed by mountain-bike riders, mostly from the Oklahoma Earthbike Fellowship. These trails are used annually for one of the state's premier mountain-bike events. Indeed, mountain-bike riders are probably more common here than hikers. But the trails provide a good venue for both activities.

After a mile or so the trail begins a northwesterly climb toward higher ground. Hikers can decide how much distance they want to cover and at what point they want to turn around and head back. About 1.5 miles from the trailhead you get a nice view of the reservoir and the rest of the park to the north and west.

The trail continues on another mile or so in a generally westerly route. The terrain gets rocky in parts and occasionally intersects with the Blue Trail and White Trail. The Yellow Trail turns south for the last mile or so to the West Area trailhead. This trailhead also marks the end (or beginning) of the out-and-back White Trail, which roughly parallels the Yellow Trail on the outside, closer to the reservoir.

Hikers who have come to the West Area trailheads via the Yellow Trail can get a different view by taking the White Trail (4.1 miles) back to the start in the East Area.

These trails traverse a region with a typical variety of southwestern Oklahoma rocks, grass, cactus, and trees. The reservoir and distant hills provide a pleasant view. The road through the park is never more than a mile from the trail, though it often stays hidden from view.

⑤ Wichita Mountains Wildlife Refuge

The Wichita Mountains cover some 1,300 square miles, extending into several counties of southwestern Oklahoma. The most impressive outcrops are in the 59,000 acres designated as the Wichita Mountains Wildlife Refuge, much of it along the north border of the Fort Sill Military Reservation. Two of the range's highest hills, Mount Gifford Pinchot (2,479 feet) and Mount Scott (2,466 feet), rise some 600 to 700 feet above the surrounding plains.

American bison and longhorn cattle roam freely and graze on the mixtures of short- and long-stemmed grasses found in the refuge. Many of the hills are thickly covered with blackjack oak trees, and the prickly pear cactus can be painful for a careless hiker. One designated campground and a number of picnic areas are open year-round. Several hiking trails cross the western side of the refuge, but they are not clearly marked in some areas. Newcomers to the refuge should stop by the well-maintained visitors' center along State Hwy 49 for maps and information.

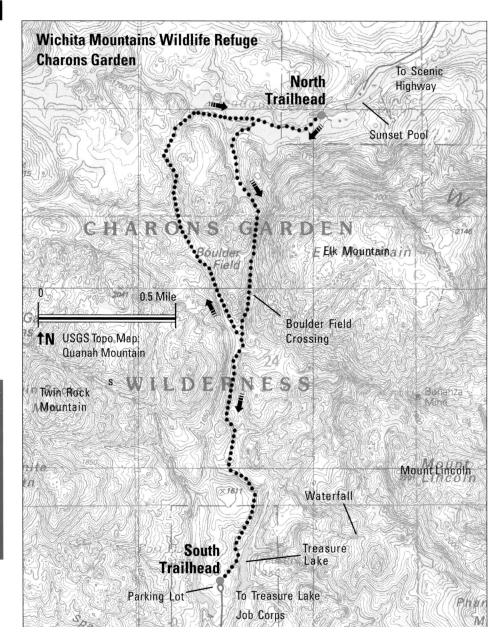

**Wichita Mountains Wildlife Refuge
Charons Garden**

North
Trailhead

To Scenic
Highway

Sunset Pool

C H A R O N S   G A R D E N

Boulder
Field

Elk Mountain

0   0.5 Mile

↑N USGS Topo Map:
      Quanah Mountain

Boulder Field
Crossing

Twin Rock
Mountain

S W I L D E R N E S S

Bonanza
Mine

Mount Lincoln

Waterfall

South
Trailhead

Treasure
Lake

Parking Lot

To Treasure Lake
Job Corps

❺ Charons Garden
North-to-South Route

LENGTH: 5 miles out and back

DIFFICULTY: Moderate/strenuous

USAGE: Hiking

SPECIAL NOTE: No water available; poisonous snakes frequent the area from spring until fall

TH GPS READING: N 34°43.823' W 98°43.601'

From I-44 turn west onto State Hwy 49 (also called the Scenic Highway) to enter the refuge. Charons Garden is about 10 miles west of the east entrance to the refuge and flanks Elk Mountain on the south and west. A sign at the edge of the woods about a quarter-mile west of the parking lot at Sunset Pool and just beyond a small spillway marks the north trailhead to Charons Garden. (The south trailhead is at Treasure Lake just north of the Job Corps facility.)

For a primitive hiking adventure and ruggedly beautiful vistas, the Charons Garden Wilderness Area ranks high. These 5,000 acres of pristine wilderness are tucked away in the southwestern corner of the Wichita Mountains Wildlife Refuge and rarely receive visitors. Hikers should be prepared for rough trails, boulder hopping, thick underbrush in summer, and eye-popping photo opportunities about every half-mile.

Two words are often used in describing the Charons Garden area: pristine and primeval. The jagged, oversized boulders in every direction give the landscape a prehistoric look.

The initially well-marked dirt trail runs west-southwest through an area of woods (still recovering from a burn) less than a half-mile before crossing a usually dry stream. For the quickest route to Charons Garden, turn sharply left just before crossing the dry stream. Look closely for the faint trail heading south-southwest. Just to the southeast looms flat-topped, steep-sloped Elk Mountain, dominating the skyline at a height of 2,300 feet.

The path skirting Elk Mountain on its west side leads directly into this wilderness. Occasional views to the west reveal Twin Peaks: a pair of egg-shaped rocks precariously balanced on a hilltop. Along the west side of Elk Mountain you can view the often-photographed Apple-Pear rock formation.

GREAT PLAINS (W)

A little more than one mile into the hike you come to a small boulder field that requires some nimble rock hopping and a stiff upper lip for most flatlanders. Caution: in the early 1990s a solo hiker was killed when he fell into one of the deep crevasses between these rocks. This boulder field is the gateway to Charons Garden.

But before beginning the series of jumps and stretches over these boulders, you should take a few minutes to enjoy the incredible view to the south and west. For several miles you can see only the rugged boulders and patches of blackjack oaks that characterize the "garden." On a sunny day in the spring or early fall this view can provide a sublime moment. Many of the locals refer to the Charons Garden area more descriptively as the "Valley of the Boulders."

Once beyond the small boulder field the trail descends into heavy brush and oak trees. As the route heads south, you can see cavelike formations of huge rocks on the left. Following a small stream farther south leads directly to Treasure Lake, which lies just north of the Job Corps facility. A less direct route to Treasure Lake sweeps southeast, passing a scenic waterfall. Take this trail—it's worth the view when the water is flowing well. The trail may be a bit hard to find, so keep your eyes peeled.

A water break on the Treasure Lake dam affords a good view of the south and southwest side of Elk Mountain. From the Charons Garden trailhead to the Treasure Lake dam is only about 2.5 miles one way, but the rough trail and boulder hopping make it seem farther.

Return by the same route or for a little variety stay on the trail that bypasses the boulder crossing on the west. Just follow this trail as it makes a clockwise loop and brings you back to the dry streambed where you turned sharply south going out.

❺ Elk Mountain

LENGTH: 2 miles out and back

DIFFICULTY: Moderate/strenuous

USAGE: Hiking

TH GPS READING: N 34°43.898′ W 98°43.402′

From I-44 turn west onto State Hwy 49 (also called the Scenic Highway) to enter the refuge. Elk Mountain lies about 10 miles west of the east entrance to the refuge. Parking is available at the Sunset Pool lot. The trail is marked by a sign near the footbridge a short distance northeast of the dam at Sunset Pool.

The rocky, well-marked trail proceeds like stair steps up the northeast side of Elk Mountain. Leading to the southeast, the trail occasionally divides and rejoins itself early in the hike. Try to stay on the most clearly marked path to avoid wasteful diversions.

The trail cuts through scrub oak and prickly pear cactus along the way. As you ascend above the surrounding terrain, take in the scenic vistas to the north and northeast. The trail becomes steeper as it winds around the large rocky outcrop on the southeast corner of Elk Mountain.

Near the top the trail passes through a wooded area. A rocky outcropping to the south comes into view as you exit the woods. The trail soon begins to bend to the west for the final climb. By pushing steadily without breaks, you can reach the summit in about half an hour.

The trail flattens on the top and ends on an outcropping of rocks. The view overlooks French Lake to the northeast, with Mount Scott visible farther in the distance.

❺ Dog Run Hollow Trail System
Buffalo Trail (Clockwise Loop)

GREAT PLAINS (W)

LENGTH: 8 miles out and back

DIFFICULTY: Moderate/strenuous

USAGE: Hiking

SPECIAL NOTE: No water available; poisonous snakes frequent the area from spring until fall

TH GPS READING: N 34°43.276′ W 98°42.184′

About nine miles west of the east entrance to the Wichita Mountains Wildlife Refuge, take the headquarters exit south off State Hwy 49 (the Scenic Highway) about a mile and turn east into the French Lake parking lot. At the east end of the lot a sign near the south end of a small metal bridge includes a map of the Dog Run Hollow Trail System.

The eight-mile Buffalo Trail stands out as the premier hike in the Dog Run Hollow Trail System on the western side of the Wichita Mountains Wildlife Refuge. It consists of three shorter hiking trails: Elk Trail, Longhorn Trail, and Kite Trail. The entire Dog Run Hollow Trail System offers a variety of fairly lush scenery in a largely secluded section of the wildlife refuge. The Buffalo Trail can be hiked clockwise or counterclockwise from the trailhead and is marked by occasional depictions of a buffalo head on small signs along the trail.

To hike the Buffalo Trail in a clockwise direction, cross the small metal bridge and turn left onto the trail. The well-marked trail starts off a bit rocky and gravelly and proceeds through blackjack oaks along the south side of French Lake. Stay to the left and close to the water as the trail crosses other small bridges and intersects with other trails in the system. The trail soon passes beside the dam on the east end of the lake and runs east alongside the water flow downstream from the dam.

The trail continues to pass a series of small dams as it skirts the south side of the creek through grass, woods, and rocks. At just under two miles the trail starts an incline through large rocks to the top of a ridge, which opens to a broad view to the east. You can see part of Mount Scott in the far distance in the east. At two miles the trail bends southward along the west edge of the creek.

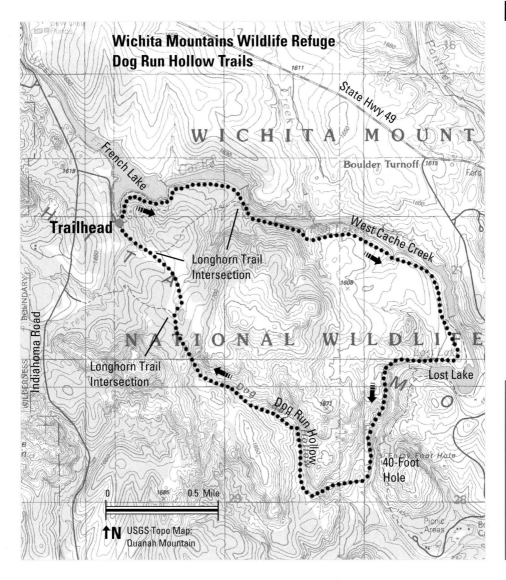

**Wichita Mountains Wildlife Refuge
Dog Run Hollow Trails**

State Hwy 49

W I C H I T A   M O U N T

Boulder Turnoff

Trailhead

French Lake

Longhorn Trail
Intersection

West Cache Creek

Longhorn Trail
Intersection

N A T I O N A L   W I L D L I F E

Indiahoma Road

Lost Lake

Dog Run Hollow

40-Foot
Hole

0   0.5 Mile

↑N   USGS Topo Map:
     Quanah Mountain

At about the three-mile mark the trail bends back to the west, still alongside the creek. It soon passes the north side of Lost Lake and continues past the distinctive native-stone dam at the west end of the lake. The trail descends sharply through large rocks to a sign depicting the trail system and your current location on the trail. This is about the halfway point of the hike and provides a good opportunity for you to get your bearing before beginning the return loop back to French Lake.

Stay on the high ground on the north and west side of the small, canyonlike depression as it bends southward. The trail becomes a little hard to follow here, and occasional subtrails lead down toward the water. During wet periods the rocky canyon below comes alive with clear rushing water, a refreshing invitation to a sweaty hiker during the summer months.

Following the canyon along the ridgeline, the trail grows faint in some sections. About a mile or so after bending southward the canyon starts to flatten out. Here the Buffalo Trail begins to meander west-northwest through Dog Run Hollow and back to French Lake. The trail becomes confusing at this point, and you may find it difficult to follow.

If you lose the trail, just keep making your way west by northwest. You'll probably pick up the trail at some point. If not, you can bushwhack without much difficulty. Just keep heading west by northwest for about three more miles until you come either to the north-south Indiahoma Road or to French Lake and its water flow east of the dam. The trail completes a full loop and ends where it starts at the small metal bridge.

The poorly maintained southwest section of the Buffalo Trail can be frustrating to follow when hiking clockwise and might be easier to hike counterclockwise. You can also hike several other shorter trails in this system, and one of them (see the map) crosses the Buffalo Trail.

⑥ Lake Arcadia

Although owned by the City of Edmond, Lake Arcadia lies just two miles west of the town of Arcadia on the fabled Route 66, America's "Mother Road." The town of Arcadia features two attractions, one old and one new: the legendary Round Barn was built in 1898 (long before the highway existed) and Pops, a soft-drink emporium, opened in 2007.

Long an iconic attraction on Route 66, the red barn is Arcadia's best-known landmark. It was built out of green lumber, soaked in water and shaped with a special jig. Many consider it an architectural wonder. In 1988 the dilapidated barn was donated to the Arcadia Historical and Preservation Society in an effort to save it from collapse. Volunteers repaired and refurbished this landmark, which is now used for parties, meetings, weddings, and other social gatherings.

Pops is the brainchild of Oklahoma City oil executive Aubrey McClendon. Designed by architect Rand Elliot, the building features a 66-foot pop bottle and houses a café and convenience store where customers can buy hundreds of brands of soda pop. The interior is decorated with soft-drink bottles arranged as displays along the wall. An instant tourist attraction, Pops recalls the old days of filling stations and drive-ins that flourished along Route 66 when it was the major highway between Chicago and Los Angeles.

The multi-use trail is located within Lake Arcadia Park and requires an entry fee.

⑥ Spring Creek Trail at Lake Arcadia

LENGTH: 7 miles one way

DIFFICULTY: Easy

USAGE: Hiking, mountain biking

TH GPS READING: N 35°38.394′ W 97°23.365′

The trailhead is located in Lake Arcadia Park at Spring Creek, which is maintained by the City of Edmond. From I-35 take 15th Street east about two miles straight into Lake Arcadia Park. Turn at the first left just past the entrance booth. About 200 yards up this road the well-marked trailhead lies on the left, marked by a large wooden sign on the west side of the access road. Parking is available on the shoulder of the road, and the park fee is $6 per car.

The approximately seven-mile multi-use trail is an irregular horseshoe around the west end of Lake Arcadia, with the longest section parallel to Second Street (Old Route 66) along the north edge of the park. The trail can be accessed at several points. The most interesting part is the section beginning at the Spring Creek Park. It is best hiked as an out-and-back while choosing your own distance.

For the most part, the well-marked trail is relatively flat and is easy to follow. A number of alternate trails splinter off the main trail. You should generally take the trails on your right, which lead you away from the perimeter of the park and into the woods. These trails offer a more interesting hike, removed from urban sights and sounds. The trail is often used for mountain biking, so be on the lookout for bikers, particularly on weekends.

Beginning at the Spring Creek Trailhead, proceed straight ahead through the woods for several hundred yards to a Y in the trail. Take the left fork. Shortly you come to a sign for Burn Out Hill, which is difficult for mountain bikers but not for hikers. Whichever trail you take here, they rejoin after a short distance.

After approximately two miles you come to Spring Creek. Continuing your hike requires a wet crossing, which can vary greatly according to the season and the level of water in the creek. You can end your hike here and return to the trailhead (a nice four-mile hike). If you continue after crossing, you parallel the creek on your left for about a quarter-mile. The trail then swings north and east until you reach a point very close to Route 66. From here the trail goes generally east, winding through the woods parallel with the highway. This is the least interesting section, in some places very close to the highway. The trail crosses two paved roads that lead from the highway into the park and ends at the parking lot at the Project Office. It is easy to pick up the trail on the other side of the paved roads because it is well marked.

Overall, the Spring Creek Trail offers a pleasant walk in the woods and a reasonable escape from the city. It is also a good trail for bird watching. Songbirds are plentiful, along with some views of the lake, with ducks, geese, and an occasional eagle or pelicans in the fall and winter if you are lucky.

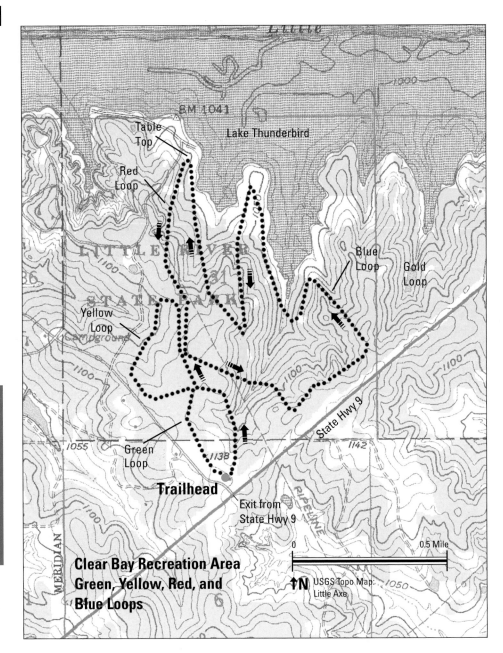

Table Top

Red Loop

Lake Thunderbird

BM 1041

Little

LITTLE RIVER

STATE PARK

Yellow Loop

Campground

Blue Loop

Gold Loop

State Hwy 9

Green Loop

Trailhead

Exit from State Hwy 9

PIPELINE

MERIDIAN

Clear Bay Recreation Area
Green, Yellow, Red, and
Blue Loops

0   0.5 Mile

↑N   USGS Topo Map:
     Little Axe

❼ Clear Bay Recreation Area
Green, Yellow, Red, and Blue Loops

LENGTH: 7-mile loop

DIFFICULTY: Easy/moderate

USAGE: Mountain biking, hiking

TH GPS READING: N 35°12.249′ W 97°14.399′

The trailhead is located in Thunderbird State Park at Clear Bay Recreation Area next to Lake Thunderbird. The entrance to the park is on State Hwy 9, 12 miles east of I-35. Turn north from Hwy 9 into the Clear Bay Recreation Area. The trailhead is about a quarter-mile ahead on your right, just past the riding stables and north of the Nature Center. The trailhead has paved parking and restrooms.

The Clear Bay Trail System was developed by the Oklahoma Parks and Recreation Department and the Bicycle League of Norman (BLN), which helps maintain the trails. The BLN has done a good job of keeping the trails in good shape for walking or biking. Most of the trail is single-track, with over 900 feet of elevation in ascents and descents.

A shelter that is easily seen from the road identifies the trailhead. On the wall of the shelter is a color-coded map, which can also be found at several locations throughout the trail system. To follow this hike, consult the map at the trailhead and be aware of the color codes. The trail is broken down into five loops: the Green Loop (1.5 miles), Yellow Loop (1 mile), Red Loop (2 miles), Blue Loop (2 miles), and Gold Loop (4 miles).

The Gold Loop has been extended by adding a number of other trails, bringing the length of the entire trail system to about 15 miles. The Gold Loop can be a good hike by itself. But hiking it is sometimes confusing because of the many side trails and loops that do not appear on either the trailhead map or the map available on the Oklahoma Earth Bike Fellowship website (www.okearthbike.com).

GREAT PLAINS (W)

This hike begins on the Green Loop. Follow it counterclockwise approximately half a mile, where it intersects the Yellow Loop. Turn right on the Yellow Loop for a brief hike to the beginning of the Red Loop. Turn right onto the Red Loop and proceed until you cross a north-south double-track. Straight ahead is the Blue Loop.

Follow the Blue Loop in a counterclockwise direction. At about two miles from the trailhead you come to an intersection with the Gold Loop. Stay to your left and follow the Blue Loop, which eventually intersects the Red Loop.

Turn right onto the Red Loop and follow it past Table Top (identified by a wooden sign) until you reach the Yellow Loop. Take the Yellow Loop to your right, which loops back to join the west part of the Green Loop and take you back to the trailhead. The entire hike is seven miles long, with a number of ups and downs and some views of the lake.

If you decide to lengthen your hike by taking the Gold Loop, a number of options are available. But be very careful to stay oriented on the Gold Loop because of its many side trails and confusing nature.

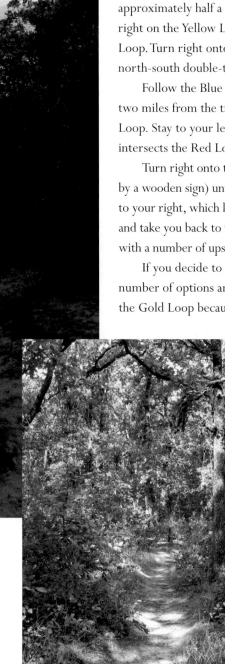

Urban Trails

Cities and towns all across the state have recognized the fitness and recreational benefits of urban trails. These mostly hard-surfaced trails provide a great outdoor recreational experience for thousands of residents daily and a way for visitors to exercise and explore Oklahoma's cities.

Both Oklahoma City and Tulsa have adopted comprehensive plans for trail systems, which are still being expanded. Other cities such as Bartlesville, Edmond, and Lawton have done likewise.

The signature urban trails in the state are Tulsa's River Parks Trails and the Lake Hefner Trails in Oklahoma City. Both of these multi-use trails are popular throughout the year with walkers, runners, bikers, and in-line skaters. They are also the venues for many kinds of organized competitive events.

As the general population becomes more aware of the health benefits of regular exercise, even more urban trails will no doubt be developed and those already in existence will be more heavily used.

❶ Lake Hefner

Oklahoma City

The most popular trail system in the Oklahoma City area is the multi-use trail that circles Lake Hefner. Used by walkers, runners, bikers, and in-line skaters, the trail creates heavy traffic on nice days, particularly on the east side of the lake and at the Stars and Stripes Park area on the south shore.

The trail is entirely paved with concrete and asphalt. The multi-purpose outside loop is 9.5 miles long, completely circling the lake, with just over three miles on the dam road. Several additional paved loops off the main trail add about one mile more for walking or running. Another 1.5 miles of trails wind through the Stars and Stripes area. On the east side of the lake the trail splits between biking and pedestrian use for about 1.5 miles. Wooden distance markers are located every half-mile all around the lake on the bike trail.

The lake is located between Hefner Road on the north and Grand Boulevard on the south. Bordered on the east by Hefner Parkway, it extends nearly to MacArthur Avenue on the west. The trail can be accessed at several points from paved parking. The East Wharf area includes restaurants and office buildings and is accessed from Britton Road. Other popular access points are at Portland Avenue and Grand Boulevard and just south of Hefner Road at the beginning of the dam. The one-way dam road proceeds west to east.

Oklahoma City maintains the trail well, with the support of many local groups. This is a far cry from 1985, when the oil bust almost derailed the whole trail concept. At that time the first 1.5-mile trail at Stars and Stripes Park had been privately funded through the Hefner Trails Organization. When the economy collapsed after the Penn Square Bank failure and donations dried up, the trail was left uncompleted. Some construction bills went unpaid, and no funds were available for maintenance.

Bert Cooper, who is the person most influential in the development of the trails, was involved with the now-defunct Hefner Trails Organization. He remembers when he and three other surviving members of Hefner Trails had to pay for mowing the area. The trail was finally completed with private donations and accepted by Oklahoma City. Appropriately, one loop of the trails is named after Cooper in recognition of his efforts in establishing the trail system.

The Hefner Trail System grew when the Oklahoma Department of Transportation financed the trails on the east side of the lake as part of the remediation required by the building of the Hefner Parkway. A city bond issue and federal funds helped pay for the extension of the Hefner Trails to the west, circling the lake in 1997.

The current facility provides an excellent place for year-round outdoor activities and is heavily utilized by both Oklahoma City residents and visitors. One of the few drawbacks is the interaction between cars and trail users, most notably at the East Wharf area and at Portland Avenue. Automobile traffic crosses the trail, so users must be alert at all times and watch out for vehicles at these and several other locations.

Although swimming is prohibited in Lake Hefner, fishing, sailing, wind-surfing, and parasailing are all popular sports. Two 18-hole golf courses, a model-airplane flying facility, and numerous baseball, softball, and soccer fields are scattered around the lake. Swings, slides, and other equipment are provided for children. This is Oklahoma City's urban mecca for outdoor sports.

It is also now possible to combine the Hefner Trails with a trail that leads all the way to Lake Overholser some five miles away. The Hefner-Overholser Trail intersects the Hefner Trails at Britton Road on the west side of the lake and then continues to MacArthur and thence southwest around Wiley Post Airport and eventually winds its way to Lake Overholser. This trail has some rough spots where it travels down Wilshire Boulevard and also crosses Northwest Highway, a major thoroughfare. If you intend to take this connecting trail, you should be aware of traffic and proceed with caution.

② **Bluff Creek**

Oklahoma City

The entrance to the Bluff Creek Trail is located just north of the intersection of Hefner Road and Meridian. There is paved parking at the trailhead.

Bluff Creek has two different trails: a paved trail a little over one mile in length and a dirt trail that winds through the woods for 3.5 miles. A kiosk with a map of the trail marks the beginning of the dirt trail. It is easy to follow, with distance markers every quarter-mile. The trail includes some short but steep descents and ascents in and out of a usually dry creek bed. Off-road bikers make heavy use of the trail, so you should be alert for them.

The Bluff Creek area changed radically in 2008 with the addition of paved parking and the paved trail. Originally established for off-road biking by the Oklahoma Earthbike Fellowship, the trail was lightly used by walkers and runners before the parking area and paved trail were added. It is now a busy spot for runners and walkers as well as bikers, particularly on weekends.

Dolese Park

Oklahoma City

Dolese Park is located at 5105 NW 50th Street, near the Putnam City High School football stadium. A dirt trail circles the entire park. A little over two miles long, the trail has a good surface for running or walking. It is protected by trees from the wind, which makes it an attractive place to exercise on a cold, windy day.

Dolese Park also has a fishing lake, a disc golf course, and the Northwest Optimist Youth Sports Complex, with soccer, baseball, and football fields. Plenty of parking in a paved lot is available near the 50th Street entrance to the park.

❹ Martin Nature Park

Oklahoma City

Martin Nature Park is a 140-acre wildlife sanctuary in northwest Oklahoma City. Open year-round from 9:00 A.M. to 6:00 P.M. on Wednesday through Sunday, the park is located at 5000 West Memorial Road. You must approach it from the west because the entrance is located on the south frontage road of Memorial Road, which is one way from west to east.

More than 3 miles of dirt and gravel trails traverse the park. It is more appropriately a place for bird watching and strolling. The trails are not designed for running or hiking but are comfortable for walking. Bird life is plentiful and varied. This interesting wildlife sanctuary is easily accessible for both adults and children.

URBAN

⑤ Oklahoma River
Oklahoma City

Not long ago, the North Canadian River running through downtown Oklahoma City was little more than a mud flat containing only a trickle of water. When water did flow down the river, it mostly carried trash. Now renamed the Oklahoma River and controlled by a series of locks and dams, the river is a desirable recreational destination and a venue for national and international rowing, kayaking, and canoeing events.

Excursion boats also travel up and down six miles of the river from Meridian on the west to Regatta Park near Bricktown in downtown Oklahoma City on the east. The Chesapeake Boathouse at Regatta Park is the focus of rowing activities, and both the University of Oklahoma and Oklahoma City University plan to build boathouses there. In addition, a state-of-the art skateboard and BMX park is located nearby in Wiley Post Park at SW 17th and Robinson Avenue.

The city has constructed 13 miles of trails along the river. Used for running, walking, cycling, and in-line skating, the trails are free of motorized vehicles. The largely flat routes stretch for seven miles along the south side of the river from I-35 on the east to Meridian on the west and for six miles on the north side of the river from I-35 to Portland. Vehicle-free crossovers are located at Portland and Robinson. Parking and trail access are at SW 15th and Meridian; River Park, SW 8th and Agnew; Wiley Post Park, SW 17th and Robinson; and SW 15th just east of Portland on the south side and at Regatta Park, off Byers Avenue just west of the Byers Avenue Bridge; SW 15th between Walker and Robinson; and Wheeler Park at SW 9th and Shartel on the north side.

Unfortunately, some caution is necessary when using these
trails. Areas of the city adjacent to the trails are not entirely safe, and
crimes have been committed against trail users. The trails are not
recommended for lone hikers or at night. The city is trying to police the
neighborhoods along the trails, but at this time users should stay alert.

⑥ NuDraper Trail
Oklahoma City

NuDraper is a pleasant trail for hiking and easily accessible from anywhere in the Oklahoma City metro area. The trail is designed principally for off-road biking but is also a good place for hiking and trail running.

Exit I-240 at Douglas Boulevard and go north on Douglas. Take SE 74th Street to Post Road and turn right (south). After less than a mile on the left you come to a gravel parking lot and a well-marked trailhead at a picnic area to the east. A good color-coded map is mounted on a wooden sign at the trailhead. You should consult the map before you begin your hike.

The trail system (about 10 miles long) is divided into three loops, color-coded green, red, and yellow. A good hike combines the Green Loop and Red Loops but can be extended by adding the Yellow Loop or shortened by leaving out the Red Loop.

For a six-mile hike combining the Green Loop and Red Loop, start to the left at the trailhead and proceed clockwise on the Green Loop. The trail is clearly marked with colored arrows on the trees. It is quite flat, well maintained, and easy to follow. This is an especially good trail for trail running: it is smooth and has very few rocks or stumps.

After a short walk on the Green Loop, you come to a double-track. Proceed to your right on the double-track and then to your left on the single-track Red Trail, which runs north and east and eventually loops back to the same double-track farther to the east. At this point signs direct you back to the Green Trail and to Terry's Turnpike. After crossing the double-track you are back on the Green Loop.

A number of whimsical signs identify sections of the trail, such as Toilet Bowl, Basket Way, and Bubba's Homestead. Although it is unclear exactly what these signs point out, they let you know you are still on the trail.

Almost six miles from the trailhead you come to another double-track. Turn to your right (west) and follow it back to the trailhead.

If you want to add an additional four miles to your hike, you can cross the double-track to the south and hike the Yellow Loop. This loop is a good example of how to create an interesting trail in a compact area. By making the trail wind around itself, the Oklahoma Earthbike Fellowship has created the feeling of covering a lot of territory by utilizing a small but interesting tract of land. Although the trail winds, you do not get the feeling of running laps or retracing your path.

Another interesting feature of the NuDraper Trail System is the presence of unique-looking rose-colored rocks in a number of locations. In some places the ground is covered with them. You can also see wildlife and bird life along the trails.

Overall, NuDraper provides an easy, enjoyable hike close to town that takes you out of the urban environment.

⑦ Lake Overholser
Oklahoma City

Built in 1919, Lake Overholser is Oklahoma City's oldest water-supply lake. It has also long been the scene of many recreational activities. Located on the western edge of Oklahoma County between Council Road on the east and Morgan Road on the west, NW 10th Street on the south, and NW 39th Street on the north, it remains a popular spot for fishing and boating and is also a good place for walking, running, and biking.

The Overholser Trail runs for over two miles along the east side of the lake from the Overholser Shelter near 10th Street to 39th Street on the north. This paved trail runs underneath NW 39th Street north to 50th Street. By traveling east on 50th Street at this point you can reach the paved trail that meanders northeast (with some connections to city streets) all the way to Lake Hefner.

At 50th Street you also reach the entrance to Stinchcomb Wildlife Preserve. A dirt road along the north edge of the preserve offers another option for walking or running.

Runners and bikers can circle the lake by utilizing the Overholser Trail on the east side and following the lake road around the lake to the sidewalk along 10th Street and then back to the Overholser Shelter. A complete circuit of the lake is just over eight miles.

Part of this is the path of historic Route 66 on the north side of the lake, crossing over the old bridge that was traversed by Andy Payne, the Oklahoma Indian who won the Bunion Derby race across America in 1928. Circling the lake is best done in the early morning, because traffic can be a problem later in the day.

A new addition to the scene is the Route 66 Park on the west side of the lake. This city park has a children's playground, picnic pavilion, three small ponds, and a paved trail about one mile long.

8 Hafer Park
Edmond

Hafer Park, located at 9th and Bryant in downtown Edmond, is an extensive urban park that features a large aquatic center, picnic pavilions, playground equipment, baseball fields, and a children's fishing pond. A paved parking lot is on the left as you enter the park from Bryant. The trail starts just across the street to the south of the parking lot.

The asphalt trail runs counterclockwise along the side of a creek for the first quarter-mile and then passes through a thick canopy of trees and greenery. The trail is mostly flat, with some minor ups and downs, a pleasant and relaxing place for a walk or a run. The loop around the park is about one mile long.

⑨ J. L. Mitch Park

Edmond

J. L. Mitch Park is located on Covell Road between Kelly and Santa Fe in north Edmond. The park, owned and maintained by the City of Edmond, is the site of baseball and softball fields, a disc golf course, a picnic pavilion, a children's playground, a skateboard park, and a senior center.

The trail circles the entire park property. It can be accessed by foot from several locations. The main entrance to the park is off Covell Road. As you enter from Covell, park in the lot immediately on your left, at the trailhead.

This is a multi-use trail with an asphalt surface. It is well marked and provides a good place to run or walk without having to deal with vehicle traffic. The trail is two miles long, with wooden distance markers. A few side trails lead to additional short loops off the main trail, which has a few hills and at one point crosses a bridge over a deep ravine bottomed by a creek. It travels mainly through open areas but in places winds through stands of trees where bird life is plentiful.

Near the end of the trail is a unique little outdoor gym equipped with what looks like playground equipment. This is actually a set of exercise machines for adults.

⑩ River Parks

Tulsa

For more than 30 years River Parks Trail has been Tulsa's premier running and walking venue. It also is heavily used by cyclists and in-line skaters.

Established in 1974 by a far-sighted group of city leaders, the River Parks encompass over 800 acres of land along the banks of the Arkansas River. The park and trail are operated by the River Parks Authority, a public trust. It has done a good job of maintaining, improving, and beautifying the parks. Fishing, rowing, and kayaking take place on the river. Children's playgrounds and picnic areas are scattered throughout the park. An amphitheater and a floating stage on the west side of the river host open-air performances and concerts.

The trail runs along the east bank of the river from 11th Street to 101st Street, a distance of over nine miles. On the west side of the river it goes 6.5 miles from 11th Street to 68th Street and connects to the Turkey Mountain Urban Wilderness Area. Water fountains and restrooms are scattered along the trail, with distance markers every half-mile. The surface of the trail is asphalt. Several paved parking lots are found on both sides of the river, and the trail is easily accessed at most points.

A pedestrian bridge crosses the river at 31st Street; more bridges with pedestrian walkways are at 11th, 21st, and 71st Streets. The trail connects on the north with the Katy Trail and on the south with the Creek Turnpike Trail. A popular loop is created between 11th Street and 31st Street by crossing and recrossing the river at the pedestrian bridge and the 11th Street Bridge.

The River Parks Trail is a good example of what can be done by a city to promote recreation and fitness in an urban setting. It provides a great escape for city dwellers and visitors to enjoy healthy exercise outdoors and a break from their jobs or business commitments.

⑪ LaFortune Park
Tulsa

LaFortune Park is located between 51st Street and 61st Street east of South Yale. This urban park offers baseball, tennis, swimming, and golf to the public and also has picnic grounds and a community center.

A nice 3.2-mile asphalt trail runs around the golf course. The trail is contained in the park and is free from vehicle traffic. This makes a good place to run or walk and is convenient for residents or visitors who may be staying in the immediate area. The trail is neither as interesting nor as long as the nearby River Trails but is adequate for a short run or walk.

A curfew closes the park from 11:00 P.M. to 5:00 A.M. The best place to park is at the paved lot just off Yale between 61st and 51st on the east side of the street.

⑫ Oxley Nature Center, Mohawk Park
Tulsa

Mohawk Park is located in north Tulsa just off E. 36th Street N, near the Tulsa International Airport. The park contains a golf course, the Tulsa Zoo, and a fishing lake. The road to the Oxley Nature Center from the park entrance is well marked. The trailhead is at the parking lot near the Interpretive Building, and trail maps are available. The parking lot is open from 8 A.M. to 5 P.M. daily; however, you may park outside the gate and hike the trails from 7 A.M. to 9 P.M.

Some of the prettiest urban trails in the state are located at the Oxley Nature Center. It contains 800 acres of heavily wooded land, with a wide variety of birds and other wildlife. A pond, a lake, a creek, and a marsh are located in the area, creating a diverse habitat. The center also includes an Interpretive Building for wildlife exhibits.

Approximately eight miles of clearly marked and well-maintained trails crisscross the area. The center is particularly good for children. All of the trails are short, but most are interconnected and can be combined for an enjoyable hike.

One of the most interesting trails is the Blackbird Marsh Trail. It circles a marsh and also leads to an observation tower overlooking Lake Sherry, providing a good place for bird watching. The lake is frequented by a variety of shore birds.

⑬ Pathfinder Parkway

Bartlesville

The Pathfinder Parkway winds 12 miles through the City of Bartlesville. This paved multi-use trail provides a good place for biking, running, walking, and bird watching.

The trail was conceived in 1971 and dedicated in 1976. In 1996 the George Miksch Sutton Avian Research Center in Bartlesville proposed that a part of the trail be designated as a bird trail. The portion of the trail between Jo Allan Lowe Park and the high school is a bird trail with signage donated by Phillips Petroleum (now Conoco/Phillips). This part of the trail also features a suspension bridge over the Caney River.

The parkway travels through Bartlesville's major parks. It is easily accessed in many places, with trailheads at Johnstone Park, Jo Allan Lowe Park, Robinwood Park, and elsewhere.

One of the most extensive and best-conceived urban trails in the state, this trail is lengthy enough for a long out-and-back walk, run, or bike ride and provides a shady place to get outside on a hot day.

⑭ Boomer Lake
Stillwater

Boomer Lake is located several miles north of State Hwy 51 (Sixth Street in Stillwater) on Boomer Road, which turns into Washington on the north end of the lake. A number of parking lots in various locations around the park area provide ready access to the trail.

This large lake offers about six miles of paved trail. While the route's hard surface seems better suited for bicycling, the lake scenery makes the hike pleasant.

At one point the trail goes out and back on a slender peninsula toward the center of the lake. It also passes by a disc golf course on the west side of the lake.

Ducks inhabit the lake and bring a little bit of nature to the urban setting.

⑮ Elmer Thomas Park
Lawton

About a mile north of downtown Lawton, Elmer Thomas Park provides several miles of cycling, jogging, and hiking trails in uneven terrain with a pleasant view of a small lake. The scenic park is situated roughly between Ferris Avenue and Cache Road between Seventh Street and Second Street.

The paved and unpaved trails wind around a first-rate disc golf course, just north of a neighborhood of older but well-maintained residences. Ample parking and a visitors' center are available.

A colony of prairie dogs appears to be established in the park, bringing a bit of wilderness to this otherwise urban setting. The trails allow good views of Lake Helen on the north side of the park. Picnic tables and an outdoor stage lie along the south side of the lake.

Although definitely within an urban setting, this park provides a safe, well-maintained venue for a variety of outdoor activities, including short but adequate trails for hiking, cycling, or running.

Kent F. Frates, an Oklahoma City attorney and writer, is the author of a novel, *Don't Never Shoot Short*; a screenplay, *Cockfight*; and a book of poetry, *The Captain and His Crew*. His historical articles for *Oklahoma Today* magazine have won awards from the Society of Professional Journalists and the International Regional Magazine Association. Frates was the editor and publisher of *Sport Source Magazine*, a statewide publication covering individual sports. An avid hiker and mountaineer, he has hiked and climbed throughout the American West.

Oklahoma City resident **Larry Floyd** grew up in Lawton, Oklahoma, and first hiked the Wichita Mountains as a Boy Scout. A member of the national Highpointers Club, Floyd has stood on the highest point in each of forty-three American states. He has worked in Oklahoma City as a business and sports journalist and editor for more than twenty years. He holds a B.A. in journalism and an M.A. in history from the University of Central Oklahoma, and has published photographs and feature articles in *Oklahoma Today*, the *Chronicles of Oklahoma*, and other national and state publications.